Sales Compensation Solutions

Andris Zoltners

Prabhakant Sinha

Chad Albrecht

Steve Marley

Sally Lorimer

ZS Associates, Inc.

This publication is designed to provide accurate and authoritative information and opinions in regard to the subject matter covered. It is sold with the understanding that the publisher and authors are not engaged in rendering legal or accounting services. If legal or accounting advice or assistance is required, the services of a competent professional in those areas should be sought.

Published by ZS Associates, Inc.
One Rotary Center
1560 Sherman Avenue
Evanston, Illinois 60201

www.zs.com

Typesetting and project management: Network Typesetting Inc.

Library of Congress Control Number: 2017942536

ISBN: 978-0-9853436-9-9

Contents

CHAPTER 1

How Selling Environment Change Affects Sales Compensation

The Challenge for Sales and Compensation Leaders

Suzanne, the head of sales operations for a large corporation, had just come out of a meeting with senior company leaders. The message at the meeting was clear: Change was coming. Suzanne and her sales operations team, with input from others, were responsible for many sales support functions, including sales compensation design and administration. Although no one specifically pointed at her during the meeting, she knew the changes discussed would have a major impact on her team's work.

It wasn't too long ago, with sales flat, that certain leaders were telling her, "We need to fix sales compensation." At the time, Suzanne questioned whether sales compensation was really the issue. Recently, in fact, sales were starting to increase, which was a positive sign. But unfortunately, at the same time, margins were slipping.

Discussion at the meeting had focused first on how the internet affected customer buying and the impact this had on the field sales force. Most customers now used the web and social media to educate themselves about product and service options and prices before engaging with the company's field salespeople. In addition, many customers placed orders on their own using the company's self-service purchasing website. The number of customers who regularly relied on field salespeople for product information and order placement was shrinking.

In response, the company was planning to restructure the sales organization. A portion of the field sales force would be replaced by an inside sales team that would handle sales to smaller, lower-volume or less-demanding customers. The inside sales team would also share responsibility with field sales for midmarket customers who preferred telephone discussions to face-to-face meetings or who sought help with internet purchasing.

At the same time, the company's expectations of the field sales organization were changing. With customers having greater access to pricing information on the internet, salespeople felt increased pressure to offer customers discounts to close deals. Profitability had dipped below market benchmarks. There was a need to make salespeople accountable not just for sales but for *profitable* sales.

Suzanne wasn't sure exactly how the restructure would work – how many field and inside sales jobs there would be and how the field and inside sales teams would work together to ensure a well-coordinated experience for customers. She also wasn't sure how the company was going to measure and share information about profitability at the individual salesperson level. What was certain, however, was that Suzanne's team would need to be involved and that a big part of the effort would involve updating the sales compensation plan to align with the new sales structure and directive.

Suzanne began to contemplate the magnitude of the work that would be required. Much of this was new to her. Up to now, sales compensation had been fairly straightforward – field salespeople earned incentives on sales to their assigned customers. With the new sales model, customer responsibility would often be shared among field sales, inside sales and the internet. It wasn't clear how to design a sales compensation plan that paid individuals fairly for their performance.

In addition, there was the issue of profitability – how to measure it and how to incorporate profitability metrics into the plan. Finally, Suzanne realized that designing the new sales compensation plan was only part of the challenge. With all the changes taking place, getting the sales force to understand and embrace the new sales model and compensation plan could be just as difficult as designing the changes in the first place.

Suzanne was excited yet anxious about the task that lay ahead. She knew her decisions could affect the future success of the sales organization, as well as her own standing in the company.

Sales Compensation in Today's Changing Business World

For sales and compensation leaders like Suzanne, creating an effective sales compensation program in today's continuously changing business environment is very challenging. Doing it right creates a double win. Salespeople win because they are appropriately rewarded for their hard work and good performance, while the company wins through a better-motivated sales team that drives results and is more likely to achieve company goals. Companies and their sales forces both benefit when the sales compensation plan is designed and implemented for maximum effectiveness.

The complexities of designing and implementing sales compensation plans today arise from several ever-evolving change forces, as illustrated in Figure 1-1.

Figure 1-1. Change Forces That Affect Sales Compensation

Market Change Forces

Constant change in the digital environment, customers, competition and the workforce is requiring companies to be more nimble and agile when developing their sales strategies. Sales processes and roles must adapt to the ever-changing world, and sales compensation plans must adapt as well to stay aligned.

The Digital World

An environment of unprecedented information technology and digital channel innovation is rapidly changing the nature of business. Advances in information technology, including systems (customer relationship management, digital asset management), tools (data management, analytics), infrastructure (mobile, cloud) and information (big data), give sales forces, along with their customers and competitors, better access to information. At the same time, digital channels (apps, social media, email, text messaging, videoconferencing) give buyers and sellers new ways to connect and create value for one another. All of these changes affect sales forces and sales compensation plans.

More Informed Customers

As access to information makes customers better informed and more self-sufficient, power is shifting from sellers to buyers. Increasingly, customers can make purchase decisions without the help of a salesperson. Still, some customers want advice from salespeople and help with sifting through the flood of information and misinformation. At the same time, there are an increasing number of global customers who desire greater efficiency in purchasing across countries. These changes in customer needs affect sales forces and the design of sales compensation plans.

Powerful Competitors

Competition is more intense than ever. Technology and the availability of information are reducing barriers to entry and making it difficult for companies to create and sustain competitive advantage. Companies are moving their manufacturing to lower-cost locations. The internet allows companies from anywhere on the globe to compete for business, often by eliminating the need for expensive distribution networks or sales teams. For companies that use a sales force to create competitive advantage, sales compensation remains a key factor in attracting and retaining sales talent.

Workforce Diversity

Managing a sales force requires addressing the needs of salespeople from different generations and career stages, as well as managing different personalities. The entry of a large number of millennial-generation workers into sales forces has introduced new diversity in terms of what motivates and engages salespeople. The millennial generation's technology savvy is an asset in today's digital environment. At the same time, this generation has new expectations about career progression and has different wants and needs from other generations in the workforce. An increasingly diverse workforce challenges companies to design sales compensation and other motivation programs that go beyond money alone as a means of engaging salespeople.

Impact on the Sales Force

Amidst all these external market challenges, sales forces remain on the hook to drive profitable sales growth. To succeed, companies must adapt their sales strategies. They must redesign sales processes and roles and rethink many sales force decisions and programs, including sales force design, customer engagement, sales force hiring and development, motivation and sales operations. In short, companies must realign all components of the sales force system to enable success in a new world, and the sales compensation plan is an important part of that effort.

Current Sales Compensation Issues

Despite all the change taking place today, sales compensation remains a powerful management tool for motivating salespeople, providing strategic direction and encouraging fiscal responsibility in a sales force. Several current issues make it more challenging than ever to design and implement effective sales compensation plans. Among these are the following:

Current Sales Compensation Plans Are Misaligned With Today's Sales Roles

As selling today is increasingly multichannel and complex, traditional sales compensation plans designed around a single sales role are no longer sufficient. Each individual salesperson has less impact on sales outcomes, and it's more difficult to measure an individual's specific contribution to every sale. This reduces the power of traditional sales force incentives to motivate and challenges companies to develop plans that encourage effective orchestration of sales activity across multiple sales team members and selling channels. Team-based selling and multichannel connections also make it difficult to pay for performance when shared customer responsibility masks the contribution of each individual to the outcome.

Sales Incentives Aren't Always Enough to Motivate Today's Diverse Workforce

Current sales compensation plans use money as the primary means of motivating salespeople. But today's workforce includes people of many different generations, cultures and personality types – factors creating diversity in terms of what motivates and engages salespeople. Addressing this diversity requires creativity in designing sales incentive compensation plans and thinking beyond cash incentives as a means of engaging a diverse sales force.

More Than Ever, Sales Forces Feel Pressure to Drive Profits, Not Just Sales

Most current sales compensation plans use a sales-based metric for determining incentive payouts. However, with the increased expectation that sales forces should deliver profits, and not just sales, the ability of a plan to direct sales effort to the right customers and products, and to sell at the right price, becomes increasingly important. Companies are challenged to take advantage of improvements in data and information systems to develop better financial metrics (for example, measures of territory profitability) and to use these metrics and other features in their incentive plans to drive more profitable sales.

Sales Compensation Is Going Global

Current sales compensation plans at many global companies differ across countries; each country has its own plan aligned with the local market, business culture, laws and data availability. Increasingly, global companies are discovering that implementation of a globalized sales compensation framework can have benefits. Sales compensation plans that are global on key dimensions, but also have features acknowledging differences across countries, can reinforce global selling models while creating efficiencies in plan management and administration.

New Analytics Create Opportunities but Also Complexity for Sales Compensation

Most companies use basic analytics to monitor their sales compensation plans. For example, they will track metrics such as actual versus budgeted spending and the percentage of salespeople making quota. They will provide feedback to the sales force on metrics such as sales and quota attainment. Advances in analytics and information systems are allowing companies to do more to enhance the impact of sales compensation plans, including more powerful and customized sales force feedback and earlier and more thorough diagnosis of plan performance. The potential for using analytics to improve sales compensation plans is considerable, yet many companies are challenged to implement initiatives effectively and therefore don't realize the full opportunity.

The Issues of Quota Setting and Plan Understanding Are Not Going Away

In the Incentive Practices Research (IPR) study[1] that ZS has been conducting for more than 10 years now, two issues come up repeatedly as top challenges for many companies. First, accurate quota setting is a perennial issue. Second, companies struggle with achieving good sales force understanding of their sales compensation plans. This lack of understanding creates a big challenge for companies seeking to get their sales forces on board with frequent plan changes in today's ever-changing world. Without careful attention to these two plan implementation issues, even the best-designed sales compensation plans cannot achieve their objectives.

Achieving Sales Force Success Requires Sales Compensation Change

The hundreds of sales forces we work with every year, along with our surveys of sales and compensation professionals, suggest that more than 75% of companies will make changes to their sales compensation plans in any given year. These ongoing plan changes help to keep sales compensation aligned with a changing business environment. Some plan changes are brought about by external market forces, such as changing customer needs or new competition. Other changes are designed to exploit new opportunities for the company, such as a product launch or entry into a new market. Still other changes are designed to give the sales force a motivational lift or to deliver better on the wide-ranging expectations of sales and marketing leaders.

Whatever the reason for changing your sales compensation plan, finding the right plan design and implementing it effectively in today's complex world is no easy task. Companies that are successful will do the following:

- create a motivated sales force with manageable turnover of sales talent
- drive high levels of quality sales effort
- achieve better financial results

The Purpose and Organization of This Book

We wrote this book to help sales leaders, and others responsible for sales compensation, design and implement plans that will drive high performance in today's changing world. The book focuses on addressing key issues and challenges that are top-of-mind among the sales and compensation professionals whom we work with. Some of these issues deal with designing and redesigning sales compensation plans in response to the changing business landscape. Other issues deal with the perpetual challenge of implementing sales compensation plans to gain sales force commitment and provide efficient ongoing support and administration.

This book complements two other books we have written on the topic of sales compensation. *The Complete Guide to Sales Force Incentive Compensation* (Zoltners, Sinha and Lorimer)[2] is a comprehensive text about sales compensation plan design and implementation and is a useful reference for readers who want more detail on specific approaches and analytics discussed in this book. *The Future of Sales Compensation* (Albrecht and Marley)[3] is a book that delivers forward-looking insights about sales compensation and is an engaging read to help readers think differently about how to design, implement, communicate and support sales compensation programs for the future.

In this book – *Sales Compensation Solutions* – the five authors have collaborated to provide actionable insights for helping you address the toughest sales incentive issues in today's changing world. Together, our three books allow readers to understand the fundamentals, apply those to the current challenges they face and start thinking about stretching to tomorrow.

The issues we chose to focus on in this book are ones that come up repeatedly in our work with clients and in executive education programs we teach, as well as through surveys, conferences and webinars that we participate in. The book is not a complete assessment of every change affecting sales forces today; rather, it focuses on a few key issues that sales and compensation professionals find very challenging to address. All of these issues have a large impact on the success of a sales compensation program.

In the book we share strategic insights, pragmatic advice and illustrative case studies from our experience (unless otherwise referenced). We seek to give you practical guidance, ideas and approaches that you can put to work immediately to design and implement a sales compensation program that works in today's selling environment. The book is organized into three sections.

Section 1: Sales Compensation Background

Section 1 provides an overview of the role of sales compensation in sales forces. It includes two chapters focusing on the basics of sales compensation theory and practice. These chapters lay a foundation for the rest of the book. Reading, or at least skimming, Section 1 provides you with context for the solutions we propose for addressing the current issues covered in Sections 2 and 3.

Chapter 2: The Role of Sales Compensation

Sales compensation can work well only when it fits within the context of your overall sales program. This chapter discusses how an effective sales compensation program aligns with all sales force decisions, programs, systems and processes around a cohesive sales strategy.

Chapter 3: Four Fundamental Decisions for Effective Sales Compensation Design

Creating a sales compensation plan starts with four key design decisions. This chapter provides advice and frameworks to help you align these decisions with your selling environment.

Section 2: Addressing Recent Sales Compensation Issues

Section 2 includes five chapters that address key sales compensation issues arising from recent market changes.

Chapter 4: Aligning Compensation With Changing Sales Roles

As companies adapt their sales processes to meet the needs of more-informed customers, sales roles are changing, and sales compensation plans must adapt accordingly. This chapter shares ideas on how to rethink sales compensation as sales roles change to reflect greater customer knowledge and self-sufficiency in the buying process, as well as the need for orchestration across multiple sales roles and communication channels.

Chapter 5: Motivating the Sales Force With More Than Money

Sales forces are made up of people with varied capabilities, experiences and needs. With large numbers from three generations in the workforce today – Baby Boomers, Generation Xers and Millennials – what motivates salespeople is affected by generational differences in addition to individual differences in salespeople's personalities and needs for achievement, social affiliation, power and ego gratification. This chapter shows how to make your compensation plan part of a broader sales force motivation program that goes beyond money to appeal to the diverse motivational needs of salespeople.

Chapter 6: Driving Profit, Not Just Sales

Companies are increasingly expecting salespeople to deliver not just sales but *profitable* sales growth. To the extent that salespeople can influence profitability by controlling the price they offer their customers or by influencing the mix of higher- and lower-margin products that they sell, this chapter shows how to rethink sales compensation plan design and metrics to align sales force effort around profit objectives.

Chapter 7: Going Global With Sales Compensation

Global consistency of sales compensation can create benefits when implemented in the right way. This chapter shares ideas about two approaches to sales compensation plan globalization:

1. **Global plan design:** It's difficult to create a single global sales compensation plan for each sales role because of the varied dynamics of selling around the world. Companies can develop global guiding principles to help countries design plans that reflect a unified company perspective, while allowing flexibility to meet local needs and acknowledge cultural differences.

2. **Centralized resources:** By providing centralized resources and expertise for helping countries design or administer plans, companies of sufficient scale can realize effectiveness and efficiency benefits, as long as there is flexibility to address local issues.

Chapter 8: Using Analytics to Boost Sales Compensation Impact

The explosion of information technology and digital channel innovation opens up tremendous opportunity for companies to use analytics to boost ongoing sales compensation plan performance. With so many tools available today, it can be tough to know where to start. This chapter shares ideas for using analytics to enhance the power of a current sales compensation plan in two ways:

1. by providing more powerful and timely performance feedback to salespeople and managers
2. by helping sales leaders stay on top of plan performance, anticipate and avoid potential problems and realize opportunities

Section 3: Addressing Perpetual Sales Compensation Issues

Two sales compensation plan implementation issues – quota setting and lack of plan understanding by the field – are perennial challenges for companies. A lack of attention to quota setting has caused many well-designed sales compensation plans to fail. Additionally, insufficient focus on change management when implementing compensation plan change often leads to a lack of plan understanding by salespeople and the failure of the sales force to embrace change. Section 3 includes two chapters that address these recurring sales compensation implementation issues.

Chapter 9: Setting Quotas That Motivate

Many sales compensation plans link payout to the achievement of territory sales or profit quotas. Despite the fact that these plans are only as good as the quotas underlying them, most companies struggle with quota setting and don't invest the necessary time to do it well. Fortunately, today's digital universe provides many industries with richer data for estimating territory potential – a key factor required for setting quotas that are motivational and fair. This chapter shows how analytics and a defined process can help address what many say is their biggest sales compensation plan implementation challenge: effective quota setting.

Chapter 10: Helping the Sales Force Embrace Compensation Plan Change

Without careful attention to change management, even the best sales compensation plan design can't succeed. This chapter shows how redesigning a sales compensation plan requires proactive strategies for:

1. gaining sales force commitment

2. encouraging and requiring ownership from your sales managers

3. managing the transition for salespeople and customers

We hope this book will provide you with many actionable ideas for aligning your sales compensation program with the realities of today's selling environment.

Endnotes

1   ZS Incentive Practices Research (IPR) study. Data are gathered annually through a survey of sales compensation professionals in multiple industries worldwide. Results are provided to participating companies.

2   Andris A. Zoltners, Prabhakant Sinha and Sally E. Lorimer, *The Complete Guide to Sales Force Incentive Compensation: How to Design and Implement Plans That Work* (New York: AMACOM, 2006).

3   Chad Albrecht and Steve Marley, *The Future of Sales Compensation* (Evanston, IL: ZS Associates, Inc., 2016).

SECTION 1

Sales Compensation Background

The next two chapters provide a basic overview of sales compensation theory and practice, thus laying a foundation for the rest of the book. Reading, or at least skimming, these chapters provides you with context for the solutions proposed for addressing the current and perpetual issues discussed in Sections 2 and 3.

Chapter 2   The Role of Sales Compensation

Understand how sales compensation fits within the context of an overall sales program and why it must align with all other sales force decisions, programs, systems and processes around a cohesive sales strategy.

Chapter 3   Four Fundamental Decisions for Effective Sales Compensation Design

Get advice and frameworks for making appropriate decisions about sales compensation structure (pay level, pay mix) and incentive plan design (performance metrics, payout formulas).

Readers who feel they already have a strong grasp of these topics will find not only some refresher material in these foundational chapters but also some new anecdotes and information. This foundation can be helpful as readers move on to the chapters in Sections 2 and 3 that address the specific issues they face.

CHAPTER 2

The Role of Sales Compensation

Sales Compensation Is Not a Cure-All

Few programs get as much scrutiny and blame as the sales compensation program when something goes awry in the sales force. No matter what ails the sales force, the compensation plan is often on the short list for potential fixes.

Consider the situation at a technology company that was not achieving its sales goal for a strategically important new product. Sales leaders felt that salespeople were not allocating enough time to the product and instead were spending too much time selling familiar and easy-to-sell products and calling on low-stress "friends and family" accounts. So the company changed the sales incentive plan. Instead of paying the same commission rate on all sales, the new plan paid a higher rate for the strategic product sales and a lower rate for all other sales.

The change didn't fully remedy the problem. Salespeople said that although they understood the importance of the new product to the company, they felt that the product was complex and hard to sell. They continued to focus on easy work at the expense of difficult but more important work. They also were frustrated that the company had "slashed" their income.

After several months of disappointing sales results following the incentive plan modification, the company initiated a number of additional changes designed to increase sales force support of the new product. These changes included:

- A revamped sales training program. The new approach focused on new competencies needed to sell the new product.

- A new product specialist role so that salespeople had a resource for bringing technical expertise to customers. The specialist role had its own recruiting profile. Some existing salespeople who fit this profile became product specialists.

- A modified recruiting profile for the original sales role, with added candidate characteristics and capabilities important for success with the new product. A few salespeople who lacked the needed characteristics were moved out of the role.

When the new incentive plan was reinforced by these additional changes, the company got the change in sales force behavior and results that it desired.

Companies will make changes to their sales compensation plans for many reasons. Some changes are designed to align compensation better with new strategies, such as entering new markets or launching products. Other changes are put in place simply to motivate salespeople to work harder and drive better results. Still other changes seek to deliver on the wants and needs of different company stakeholders:

- Salespeople want a plan that's simple and fair and that pays well.

- Sales leaders want a plan that drives high levels of achievement.

- Sales operations leaders want a plan that's easy to implement and support.

- Human resource leaders want a plan that attracts, motivates and retains the best sales talent.

- Marketing leaders want a plan that focuses sales activity on the right products and markets at the right price.

- Finance leaders want a plan that's fiscally responsible.

Delivering on all these wants and needs can be challenging. Quite often, company stakeholder objectives are at odds with one another. For example:

- Sales leaders may want a plan that drives high levels of achievement by setting high target payouts with steep payout curves, but finance may believe such a plan is fiscally irresponsible.

- Marketing may want a plan that directs sales effort to many detailed brand strategies and imperatives, but sales operations may believe such a plan is too difficult to implement and support.

- Salespeople may want a plan that's both simple and fair, but these objectives often compete. For example, it's simple to pay on sales, but not all territories may have an equal market opportunity to drive sales.

Despite these complications, compensation is a familiar and relatively low-effort fix for companies. Incentive plan design changes can often be implemented quickly and with minimal disruption to the sales force structure and to customers. Many alternative fixes are more intrusive, involving restructuring the sales force, reassigning customers or changing the people on the sales team – actions likely to create disruption for salespeople and customers. In addition, incentive plan changes usually have an immediate impact on sales activity, while other solutions take more time to implement and produce results.

Too often, companies rely on incentives as the main answer for sales force challenges that can't be fully addressed with incentives alone. *At least half of the time* when sales leaders seek our help with redesigning a sales compensation plan, the solution required to address the underlying concern requires doing more than just changing the compensation plan. As the technology company example at the start of this chapter shows, compensation plan changes have more power when they reinforce changes to other sales force decisions and programs.

This chapter will discuss the role of sales compensation within the context of the broader sales force system. Then it will highlight several issues that companies frequently misdiagnose as sales compensation issues and will demonstrate how, by reinforcing other sales force solutions with simultaneous compensation plan changes, companies can realize a more significant and lasting impact on sales force performance.

Sales Compensation and the Sales Force System

Figure 2-1 shows six categories of sales force effectiveness drivers. These are the decisions, programs, systems and processes within the sales force system that have an impact on sales success.

Driving results through the sales force system requires managing all six of these categories:

1. **Sales strategy:** identifying the right markets and market segments for realizing the best growth opportunities with a differentiated and valuable offering

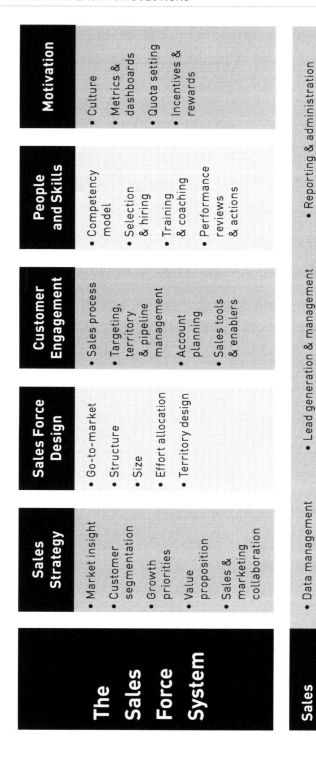

Figure 2-1. Effectiveness Drivers in the Sales Force System

2. **Sales force design:** sizing and structuring the sales force to enable effective and efficient coverage of opportunities

3. **Customer engagement:** defining, planning and executing a customer-focused sales process maximizing mutual value and trust

4. **People and skills:** recruiting the right sales talent and developing salespeople and managers to excel in their roles

5. **Motivation:** creating a performance-focused and accountable sales force committed to getting it done and doing it right

6. **Sales operations:** efficiently supporting capabilities across all of these categories and providing the information the sales force needs to achieve superior performance

Sales incentive compensation is part of the motivation category, and it is only one piece of what drives sales force success. A sales compensation program will have maximum impact when the sales system has the following two characteristics:

1. **Excellence:** Sales compensation programs are most effective when the entire sales force system is excellent. This means that in addition to the right sales compensation plan, a company needs the right sales strategy, an appropriate sales force design, a compelling customer engagement process, talented people with the right skills, strong motivation programs to supplement the compensation plan and efficient and effective sales operations.

2. **Alignment:** Sales compensation programs are most effective when all sales force decisions, programs, systems and processes mutually support one another. In addition to being excellent, all six categories of sales force effectiveness drivers must align around a common strategy. Health in a sales force system is much like health in a natural ecosystem; it depends on overall balance. Thus, sales compensation solutions are more potent when they are compatible with and supported by the rest of the system.

Seeking Comprehensive Solutions

Companies can address challenging sales force issues by finding solutions within the portfolio of sales force effectiveness drivers. Here are examples of issues your company might face:

Customer needs have changed.
- Customers want to purchase on their own over the internet.
- Customers have new expectations that salespeople will help them solve complex business problems.
- Customer coverage is inadequate in some sales territories.

Sales force capabilities and motivation are lagging.
- It's difficult to attract good sales talent.
- Turnover of good salespeople is too high.
- Sales force morale is low because of perceived unfairness in pay.
- Sales managers aren't coaching and managing their people effectively.
- Some members of the sales force aren't motivated by the current incentive programs.

Sales force activity isn't aligned with strategy.
- Salespeople are spending too much time with "friends and family" and not enough time developing new business.
- Some profitable and strategically important customers and product lines aren't getting enough sales force attention.

Results aren't living up to expectations.
- Sales growth has slowed.
- The sales force doesn't feel accountable for poor results.

Addressing these and other sales force productivity challenges requires multiple solutions. The questions and examples provided here can help you look beyond the compensation plan to develop complete solutions for driving sales force improvement.

Ask the Right Questions

Figure 2-2 lists sample questions to ask to help you identify ways to reinforce a compensation plan change with a broader solution for addressing any sales force issue.

Find Solutions Beyond Sales Compensation

Asking questions (such as those listed in Figure 2-2) allows companies to look beyond the compensation plan when addressing sales force issues.

Category	Questions
Sales Strategy	• **Market insight:** Are you providing useful information to understand customers and develop the value proposition? • **Customer segmentation:** Are market segments meaningful and relevant for differentiating sales actions? • **Value proposition:** Are value propositions compelling and tailored to customer needs?
Sales Force Design	• **Sales force structure:** Does your structure enable effective and efficient selling? Do you need specialists for key products, markets or sales activities? • **Sales force size:** Do you have the optimal number of salespeople? • **Territory design:** Do territories align with customer coverage needs? Is market potential distributed appropriately among salespeople?
Customer Engagement	• **Sales process:** Is selling well matched to the customer buying process? • **Targeting:** Do salespeople have information for targeting the right customers with the right offerings? • **Sales tools & enablers:** Do salespeople have what they need to enhance the sales process and deliver what customers value?
People and Skills	• **Selection & hiring:** Are you recruiting the best sales and managerial talent? • **Training & coaching:** Are you developing salespeople for success? • **Performance reviews & actions:** Are managers providing salespeople with the right feedback and strategies for improvement?
Motivation (Other Than the Incentive Plan)	• **Culture:** Is your sales culture aligned with customer, company and sales force interests? • **Quota setting:** Are sales quotas challenging, attainable and fair?
Sales Operations	• **Analytics:** Are you using data and analytics to support ongoing sales force needs, diagnose concerns and opportunities and design excellent sales force programs? • **Lead generation & management:** Are you providing the best leads to the sales force? • **Reporting & administration:** Are your sales force support processes effective and efficient?

Figure 2-2. Questions for Reinforcing Compensation Plan Change With Broader Sales Force Solutions

By implementing improvements across multiple sales force decisions and programs, companies are creating powerful solutions with lasting impact on sales force success. Consider these examples.

Medical Devices: Aligning Sales Territories for Success

Quite often, companies blame the incentive plan for problems that are created by territories with unequal opportunity.

At a medical device company, a significant portion of salespeople's earnings came from commissions, starting with the first dollar sold. Sales force morale was quite low because many salespeople felt that differences in incentive pay were unfair and did not accurately reflect true performance differences. Some salespeople worked hard and struggled to earn a living. At the same time, these salespeople watched some of their colleagues make four times the incentive target pay without having to work especially hard.

Sales managers and leaders also observed the lack of pay for performance. They felt the skills, capabilities and motivation of the bottom 10 salespeople, who earned an average of just $31,500 in incentive pay, did not appear to be substantially different from those of the top 10, who earned an average of $128,000 in incentive pay. At the same time, sales managers and leaders felt that customers in some territories were not getting adequate coverage.

The company analyzed the demographic characteristics of each salesperson's territory by using factors such as the number of hospitals, admitted patients, surgical beds and procedures. It discovered that there were vast differences in opportunity across territories and that poor territory design was a major contributor to the variation in payout and customer coverage.

The company faced a tricky situation. Although poor territory design was the core problem, high-earning salespeople would certainly fight to keep accounts in order to keep their earning opportunity as high as possible. The company didn't want to "penalize" individuals who had developed a large business by reducing the size of their territories and, therefore, cutting their commission checks. However, by taking some accounts that were not getting sufficient coverage out of territories with large opportunity and reassigning those accounts to salespeople who had time to cover them, overall sales and attention to customers could improve dramatically.

The company changed the incentive plan so that incentive payout varied less with territory size. The new plan gave each territory a sales quota reflecting territory opportunity and paid a fixed bonus to salespeople who achieved their quota. The plan continued to pay salespeople commissions on all sales from the first dollar sold, but at a lower rate. The quota-based component of the plan reduced the impact of territory size on incentive pay and made it easier to redesign sales territories without cutting salespeople's income as much.

The company developed a plan to reassign underserved accounts in territories with large opportunity to salespeople who had less territory opportunity and therefore had more time to cover these accounts. The goal was to give all salespeople a fairer opportunity to succeed. Some of the account assignment changes were implemented right away; others were phased in over time so that salespeople in large-opportunity territories who were true strong performers would not experience a sudden income loss. In time, opportunity became more equitably distributed across territories. It took some time for the sales force to embrace the change, but eventually, sales force morale and motivation improved, as did customer and prospect coverage.

Insurance: Recruiting the Right Salespeople and Developing Them for Success

Sometimes the compensation plan gets blamed for problems that exist largely within sales force recruiting and development programs.

An insurance company paid salespeople entirely through a commission on sales. Once a salesperson sold to an account, that salesperson kept the account permanently and earned an annuity over time. The company recruited thousands of new salespeople every year. It understood that many new recruits would discover quickly that they were unsuited for the job and would leave. While the market was growing, along with company sales and profits, the company tolerated the fact that more than 60% of new recruits would leave within their first year.

As market growth slowed and sales became harder to come by, company leaders began to focus more on sales force productivity. Attraction of good people became increasingly difficult. Market conditions made it hard for new salespeople to make a living. At the same time, as a new generation of workers entered the workforce, there were fewer job candidates willing to take a totally commissioned sales job. Recruiting got tougher, too many salespeople with long-term potential left quickly and the company was squandering its recruiting and training investments because not enough employees stayed long enough to produce results.

The company considered adding a small salary component to the pay plan for new salespeople but eventually decided this could compromise the sales-oriented culture. Instead, the company implemented the following changes:

- created a more targeted recruiting profile for screening job candidates to improve the quality of new recruits

- developed an improved training and coaching program to help new salespeople get off to a faster start

- gave new salespeople a few existing customer accounts with good growth potential to help them get started (while at the same time protecting the income opportunity of existing salespeople)

By focusing beyond the compensation plan, the company successfully reduced new salesperson turnover to below the industry average within two years, thus driving sales force productivity improvements.

Office Products: Encouraging Sales Managers to Coach

Too frequently, we see sales forces directing sales force behavior by using the incentive plan rather than requiring sales managers to coach performance.

An office products distributor had for years paid its salespeople entirely through commissions on sales. New salespeople, after completing basic product training, would get a copy of the commission schedule, a list of prospects for their territory and a manager's encouragement to "go sell!" Sales managers got commissions on their own sales plus the sales of the people they managed.

Wanting to maximize their own income, sales managers saw little benefit to coaching and developing the capabilities of their people for the long term. Instead, they spent time selling to their own customers. When they visited customers with salespeople, they often jumped in to close sales themselves rather than coaching salespeople on how to do it. During annual performance reviews with their salespeople, managers focused on results, with only a superficial mention of what capabilities and activities could better drive results. Too often, the only coaching advice salespeople got from their managers was, "You need to sell more."

The entirely commission-based sales plan worked well for many years while the market was growing. As growth slowed down and new competitors came on the scene, sales got harder to come by. Clearly, salespeople and the company could benefit if managers would spend more time coaching salespeople on how to succeed in a more competitive environment, yet because managers earned commissions on their own sales, most chose to focus on selling rather than coaching.

The company made several changes to address the situation. It started by adapting the pay plan to include a salary component and putting in place quota hurdles that salespeople and managers had to reach before commissions kicked in. The new pay plan acknowledged that salespeople and managers had responsibilities that went beyond simply driving short-term sales.

To support the pay plan change and enable more effective selling in the new environment, the company also put the following in place:

- a defined sales process reflecting selling best practices, with best-practice sharing sessions that allowed salespeople to propagate ideas

- new coaching and performance management processes that required managers to emphasize salesperson behaviors and capabilities in addition to results

- new data and tools to help salespeople be more systematic and effective while working with customers

Implementing the new sales approach had its challenges, and several salespeople and sales managers who didn't buy in to the changes left the company. But company leaders were diligent in their efforts to bring about change, and, in the end, the new approach improved productivity dramatically and drove continued sales growth.

Technology Products: Creating a Sales Culture That Breeds Success

Sales compensation plan changes have minimal impact if the sales culture is not aligned for success.

Salesperson turnover at a technology products company was significantly above the industry average, and it was becoming increasingly difficult to hire good sales talent. The consensus among sales leaders was, "We need to pay more." So the company increased pay, bringing it into the top third of the industry according to the latest pay level benchmarks. The move raised sales force costs significantly but had only a minor impact on salesperson attraction and retention. The problem went beyond the sales compensation program and was rooted in the entire sales force culture. Over many years, a lack of strong sales leadership had allowed a "victim" culture to develop within the sales organization. A cynical attitude pervaded, and no one felt accountable for results. Too many salespeople were disengaged and made excuses for poor performance. The few salespeople who were successful showed little loyalty to the company.

Top executives brought in a new sales force leader who possessed values and a work style that were consistent with a more accountable and results-focused sales culture. One of the new leader's first priorities was to upgrade the sales management team, bringing on new managerial talent that possessed the right values and work style as well. It took many months for these changes to have an impact, but in time, the leadership change, when coupled with a competitive pay plan, led to significant improvements in sales force attraction and retention.

Conclusion

Compensation solutions alone are rarely sufficient to address the complex issues sales forces face. Figure 2-3 summarizes the many and varied changes the companies mentioned in this chapter implemented in order to improve their situations.

As you rethink your sales compensation program in today's changing world, consider how compensation plan changes fit within the context of the entire sales force system. Compensation is just one important way to influence salespeople and their activities, and it is essential to get that piece right. But the best sales force performance comes when all components of the sales force system, including the sales compensation plan, align with one another around a cohesive sales strategy.

	Summary of Issues from Chapter Examples	Compensation Solution	Other Solutions Reinforcing the Compensation Plan
Medical Devices	• Low sales force morale due to unfairness in pay • Lack of pay for performance • Poor account coverage in some territories	• Improve fairness by reducing commission rate and adding a bonus for achieving a territory quota reflecting territory opportunity	• Phase in sales territory design changes to improve fairness and customer coverage
Insurance	• Poor attraction of sales talent • Excessive turnover of new salespeople	• None	• Change the recruiting profile • Improve new salesperson training and coaching • Give new salespeople warm leads to help them get started
Office Products	• Lack of coaching by sales managers • Insufficient sales growth	• Add a salary component of pay • Require salespeople to reach quota hurdles before commissions start	• Implement a sales process reflecting best practices • Emphasize sales manager coaching and performance management • Provide data and tools to help salespeople work with customers
Technology Products	• Poor attraction and retention of sales talent • Lack of sales force accountability	• Increase pay level	• Bring in a new management team to implement many sales force changes and lead by example • Transform the culture and make the sales force accountable for results

Figure 2-3. Summary of Solutions at Four Example Companies

CHAPTER 3

Four Fundamental Decisions for Effective Sales Compensation Design

Sales Compensation Design Solutions

Although sales compensation is rarely a complete solution for the issues sales forces face, it's often an important part of the solution. Getting sales compensation right requires making four key decisions about the pay structure and incentive design. These decisions, as shown in Figure 3-1, are not the only decisions you'll need to make. There are logistical decisions about the incentive plan, such as who is eligible, what the performance period is and how frequently to pay incentives. There are also implementation decisions, such as how to communicate the change and update operational support systems and processes. But the four key decisions listed in Figure 3-1 form the core of your sales compensation design.

This chapter shares frameworks and advice for helping you make these four key sales compensation plan decisions. In doing so, the chapter provides a foundational reference for the topics discussed in subsequent chapters of the book. A sales compensation program with the right pay level, pay mix, metrics and payout formula is an important part of many solutions for addressing the issues your sales force may be facing.

Setting the Pay Structure

The first two key sales compensation plan design decisions – pay level and pay mix – define the basic structure of your sales compensation program.

Compensation Element	Decision	Questions and Choices
Pay Structure	Pay level	• How much should you pay salespeople?
	Pay mix	• What percentage of pay should be salary versus incentive?
Incentive Design	Metrics	• What business outcomes are you trying to drive – for example, revenue, margin or market share? • How will you measure performance of those outcomes – for example, growth or goal attainment? • How many metrics will you use, what is the weight on each one and should there be any linkages between metrics?
	Payout formula	• How will you pay for the performance achieved – for example, a commission on sales volume or a bonus based on a salesperson's ranking? • What features should you include in the payout formula – for example, payout rates for different levels of achievement, threshold at which payout begins, accelerators and decelerators or caps?

Figure 3-1. Four Key Decisions for Sales Compensation Design

Decision 1: Pay Level

The right pay level ensures your sales compensation plan is fiscally responsible while attracting and retaining strong sales talent. The right target pay level for a sales role reflects the value of the role and usually acknowledges market benchmarks.

Valuing a Sales Role: An Example

The value of a sales role depends on the skills and experience needed for the role, as well as the impact the role has with customers. Compare, for example, two sales roles at a company that sells online advertising: key account salesperson and inside sales.

Key account salespeople are responsible for navigating complex buying processes and selling large strategic deals to the company's largest customers. They affect a large volume of business. In fact, a single major win can exceed a key account salesperson's annual performance objective, and a single loss can spell trouble for the company.

Inside salespeople at this company are typically charged with closing deals with many small and medium-sized customers. Rarely would an inside salesperson see make-or-break performance from a single customer.

These two roles require different skills and experience and have varied customer and company impact, so the roles have different pay levels. Target pay for key account salespeople is approximately 2.5 times target pay for inside salespeople at this company.

Using Market Benchmarks to Determine Sales Role Value

Market benchmarks can help you determine what you'll need to pay in order to attract and retain people with the skills and experience needed for a particular sales role. Paying above market gives you competitive advantage in recruiting and retaining sales talent but can lead to high costs, sales force complacency and low turnover among poor performers. Paying below market gives you a cost advantage but can make it difficult to attract and retain good talent and can be demotivating to the sales force. Company sales could suffer.

External market surveys are available in many industries for benchmarking both salary (fixed) and incentive (variable) pay for most sales roles. Some surveys are cloud based, providing access to real-time data reflecting the latest economic and industry conditions. There are times when it's difficult to find exact external benchmarks – for example, when industry shifts lead to the creation of new sales roles and job descriptions. In such cases, it's often possible to find a similar role or job description for which benchmarks do exist. You can also gather data for benchmarking pay from salespeople who are leaving your company for comparable jobs or from new salespeople joining your company from similar roles elsewhere.

Companies have different strategies for setting pay levels relative to the industry. Some seek to lead the industry as a means of attracting and retaining top sales talent. Others prefer to emphasize other job features besides pay, such as opportunity for advancement or an appealing culture. Several years ago, Southwest Airlines[1] reportedly provided employees with a total compensation package slightly below that of other airlines. It competed for talent by emphasizing the experience of working in the company's unique culture of teamwork, fun and empowerment.

Most benchmarking surveys show pay by percentile (for example, the 90th, 50th and 10th percentile of pay). To reinforce a pay-for-performance culture, consider paying your top performers at or above what the industry pays top performers, your average performers at the industry median, and low performers at or below what the industry pays low performers. The distribution of pay across the sales force can be as important as the average pay level.

Decision 2: Pay Mix

The right pay mix – the split between salary and incentive pay – ensures your sales compensation plan pays for performance and motivates high levels of sales activity. Pay mix is expressed as a ratio – a 75:25 mix means the target is for 75% of total pay to be salary and 25% to be incentive. Pay mix affects the variation in pay across salespeople; the higher the incentive portion of the mix, the higher the potential for differentiating pay among salespeople on the basis of their current sales performance.

Conventional wisdom suggests incentive pay makes a sales force more motivated, performance focused and financially successful. However, there are two primary conditions that suggest when a company should make the incentive portion of the pay mix small:

1. **Difficulty measuring performance:** The company can't accurately measure performance at the individual salesperson level.
2. **Limits on influence:** The opportunity for individual salespeople to influence sales is restricted.

In addition, industry norms and company philosophy can play a role in pay mix decisions.

Difficulty Measuring Performance

An old management adage says, "If you can't measure it, you can't manage it." That adage, in the world of sales compensation, translates to, "If you can't measure it, you can't pay incentives on it." If you lack data for measuring sales at an individual salesperson level, your pay mix should favor salary. Consider two examples.

One company launching a new technology product wanted to prime the market by calling on potential customers before the product hit the shelves. Because there were not any sales to track, the company paid salespeople mostly salary and tied a small incentive to a management by objectives (MBO) component. Salespeople worked with their managers to set specific competency- and activity-based MBOs, and managers evaluated salespeople on their achievement. Several months after the product launch when sales data became available, the pay mix shifted to a larger incentive portion.

A manufacturer of industrial electrical components had salespeople who sold to potential customers but used third-party distributors to ship the products. The manufacturer had historically been unable to obtain consistent and reliable data for tracking sales from some distributors. It paid salespeople a large salary portion and relied on sales managers to keep salespeople's performance on track. Once all distributors began providing the company with sales tracking data, the company increased the incentive portion of pay.

Limits on a Salesperson's Ability to Influence Sales

For incentives to motivate, salespeople must be able to influence sales outcomes through their efforts. At least four circumstances can reduce an individual salesperson's influence. These circumstances include the following:

1. non-sales force factors (such as advertising) influencing customers

2. team selling

3. non-selling responsibilities (such as customer service)

4. long sales cycles (which reduce ability to influence current year results)

Non-sales force factors. Customers are often influenced by many factors besides the salesperson when making purchase decisions. For example, advertising, social media and internet searches can have considerable impact on customer purchasing. When these influences are important, an individual salesperson's skill and effort have less impact on sales, making incentives less relevant. Consider two situations:

- **Situation A:** A company sells thousands of different industrial parts and supplies. Most sales occur online without involving a salesperson, as customers search the company's online catalog, locate products and place orders. On occasion, customers will call an inside salesperson to ask clarifying questions and ensure the parts they order are the right fit. The inside salesperson is encouraged to probe the customer's needs and sell add-on products, if appropriate.

- **Situation B:** A company sells a new customized business software package. Many competing products are available. Closing a sale requires a multistep sales process. The salesperson meets directly with a potential customer several times to assess the customer's needs, describe the differentiating product features, answer questions and develop a customized solution.

In situation A, the sales compensation plan has an 85:15 pay mix. Most of the sales process is handled by customers on their own, enabled by the internet. The salesperson has minimal influence on most sales. In situation B, the pay mix is 50:50. The ability to drive business is more heavily under the salesperson's control.

Team selling. Team selling can diminish an individual salesperson's ability to influence customer buying decisions. For example, a sales force at a technology company had account managers who managed relationships with major accounts. The account managers worked with an account team of product and technical sales specialists and relied on team members to perform various selling tasks tailored to each account's needs. Each team member contributed to the sale, so individual account managers had only a partial influence on the outcome, and the exact value of their contribution was impossible to measure. The team got an incentive based on the overall outcome, but this created two problems the company had to manage. First, there were a few free riders – non-performing members of the sales team who benefited from the actions of the productive members. Second, the formula for dividing credit among team members was complex. Most salespeople didn't totally understand it, and this diminished the motivational power of the incentive. For these reasons, this company chose to revise the pay mix to include mostly salary and a small team-based incentive.

Responsibilities other than selling. Sales force time spent with customer-service or non-customer-focused activities diminishes a salesperson's ability to influence short-term sales. For example, a technology company had two primary sales roles – hunters and farmers. Hunters were dedicated to finding and acquiring new customers. Farmers performed both sales and service activities for cultivating and growing relationships and generating repeat business with current customers. Farmers were important for sustained success with customers but had less impact (compared with hunters) on immediate sales outcomes. The sales compensation plan for hunters had a 50:50 pay mix, while the mix for farmers was 70:30.

Long sales cycles. When sales cycles are long and salespeople generate only a few large transactions per year, they have limited ability to influence what sales will occur in a short time. A large incentive portion could lead to significant income variation from paycheck to paycheck. A large salary portion reduces this variation and helps reinforce the long-term, customer-focused culture needed for success with long-term sales.

Industry Practice and Sales Culture

Some industries tend to pay salespeople mostly salary. For example, in the pharmaceutical industry, the typical sales force pay mix was 75:25 in 2016, according to ZS surveys[2] and consulting experience. Other industries (for example, insurance) tend to offer a larger incentive portion. Understanding industry practice when setting pay mix has two advantages. First, it provides a good model of what pay mix works for other companies facing similar selling situations. Second, knowing how your pay mix compares with the industry's can help you set a pay mix that enhances your competitiveness in the labor market for salespeople. Some sales forces choose to match the industry mix, while others choose to deviate intentionally from the typical mix. The decision depends on your philosophy and desired culture.

As an example, both IBM and Digital Equipment Corporation (DEC) were successful computer companies in the 1980s, but, reportedly, their pay mix strategies differed significantly. While IBM paid its salespeople a roughly 60:40 split, DEC had a pay mix of 100:0. IBM's

40% incentive component encouraged a pay-for-performance sales culture. Ken Olsen, the founder and president of DEC, wanted his compensation program to align with a culture of technical problem solving for customers. Despite differences in sales culture and pay mix, both DEC and IBM had successful sales forces for many years during the heyday of mainframe and minicomputers.

Many factors can influence a sales force's culture, including company history, the selling environment and the people and leaders of the sales force; the sales compensation plan is just one contributing factor. The right compensation plan and pay mix reinforce the culture you desire. A larger salary portion of pay reinforces a sales culture focused on the long-term welfare of customers and the company. A larger incentive portion reinforces a close-now sales culture for driving short-term operating results. Either of these cultures can be effective, depending on your situation and objectives.

Designing the Sales Incentive Plan

With your sales compensation pay structure in place, the next two key decisions focus on designing the incentive portion of your sales compensation plan. This involves selecting metrics that align with desired business outcomes and designing a payout formula to motivate the right sales activity.

Decision 3: Metrics

Incentive plan metrics help to align salespeople's activities with company goals while ensuring fair payouts for everyone. Metrics should link to desired business outcomes, such as revenue, margin and market share. There are also many choices for how to measure the performance of each metric. For example, you can measure growth or improvement from the prior year, or you can measure performance relative to a goal or quota.

Incentive plans often include multiple metrics, so in addition to deciding which ones to use, it's important to determine how many to include and the relative weight on each. You can also include incentives for achieving strong performance on multiple metrics simultaneously (for example, you might offer an extra bonus to salespeople who make their quota in every product category).

Using Best Practices for Selecting Metrics

Figure 3-2 lists several best practices for choosing incentive plan metrics.

	Best Practice	Rationale
Metrics Must Be ...	... strategic	• Metrics should align salesperson behavior with strategic, business-critical goals that are relevant to the sales role.
	... measurable	• To motivate, metrics must accurately measure performance at the appropriate level and time.
	... within the salesperson's control	• For metrics to motivate, salespeople must believe they can influence the metrics.
	... linked closely to the sales "event"	• Timely rewards are more motivating – pay when the customer signs the contract, not when the customer pays, unless collections are an issue or salespeople are pursuing customers they think won't pay.
	... limited to 3 (ideally), 4 maximum	• A simple, focused plan is memorable and keeps sales force attention directed toward strategic priorities.
Minimum Weight	15%–20%	• Any metric weighted less than 15% will not be noticed by salespeople.
Type of Metric	Pay on results, not on activities	• Activities are hard to measure – people self-report when it's convenient and may misreport what they actually do. • Tracking activity often motivates an increase in quantity but also a decrease in quality. • A sales incentive plan does not replace performance management.

Figure 3-2. Best Practices for Selecting Incentive Plan Metrics

Encouraging the Right Effort Allocation

If you want to encourage salespeople to go beyond selling pure volume, the right metrics can keep salespeople focused on the strategically appropriate products, customers, selling activities and price. Figure 3-3 provides several examples.

Paying Incentives on Customer Satisfaction Metrics

Paying salespeople on customer satisfaction metrics is appealing as a means of aligning the interests of salespeople and customers. These metrics are usually based on scores from post-sale surveys asking customers to rate a product, company or salesperson on relevant dimensions. Net Promoter Score® (NPS) has gained a lot of traction, especially among technology companies, as a simple and actionable metric for measuring customer satisfaction and loyalty, although few companies tie sales incentives to this metric. To calculate NPS, ask customers a single question: How likely are you to recommend this product, service, company or salesperson to a colleague or friend? Take the percentage of people who are promoters (rating of 9 or 10) and subtract those who are detractors (rating of 1 through 6) to get the percentage of net promoters.

NPS and other customer satisfaction metrics are useful to track and provide as feedback to salespeople through the performance management process, but in most cases, customer satisfaction metrics are not appropriate for sales incentive compensation plans. There is simply too much incentive for salespeople to chase high ratings through means not in the company's and customer's best interest. It's not uncommon for salespeople to "buy" a score by promising customers free merchandise or even price discounts in exchange for positive ratings. One automobile dealer offered a free tank of gas in exchange for giving the dealership all five-star ratings. Customer satisfaction metrics can provide useful feedback for improving performance, but be wary of *paying* on customer satisfaction!

Keeping It Simple

Using just a few metrics in an incentive plan makes the plan memorable and keeps salespeople focused on what's important. With too many metrics, salespeople may get confused or may find ways to game the plan to make money without engaging in activities aligned with company

Consideration	Objective	Examples
Products	... selling the right products	• Pay more for strategic products. • Pay incentive for cross-selling. • Pay kicker for solution sales.
Accounts	... to the "right" customers	• Pay more for new customer sales. • Pay bonus for customer retention, renewal or win-back.
Orders	... in the right way	• Pay more for larger order size or longer contract length.
Profit	... at the right price or margin	• Pay on gross margin (%, $). • Pay on average selling price.
Customer Satisfaction	... resulting in a happy customer	• Pay on customer satisfaction or NPS.

Figure 3-3. Linking Incentive Pay to Metrics Encouraging Selling Effectiveness

strategy. In most cases, having three or fewer metrics in an incentive plan is recommended for driving the best performance.

Decision 4: Payout Formula

A good payout formula motivates high levels of the right kinds of sales activity while paying for performance and ensuring fiscal responsibility. The payout formula defines the relationship between a salesperson's performance on the selected metrics and the incentive payout received. Examples include the following:

- The salesperson earns a percentage of target incentive pay based on the percentage of quota achieved.

- The salesperson earns a commission on the gross margin dollars generated. The commission percentage can vary across products, customers or ranges of results.

- The salesperson earns a bonus determined by performance ranking relative to peers.

Payout formulas are often shown graphically. For example, Figure 3-4 shows a graph of a payout formula for a plan in which salespeople earn a salary plus a commission on sales, with the commission rate tied to their territory quota achievement. For more payout formula and graph examples, see *The Complete Guide to Sales Force Incentive Compensation* (Zoltners, Sinha and Lorimer).[3]

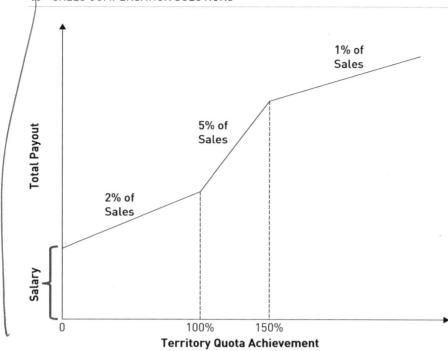

Figure 3-4. Payout Formula Example

Payout formula graphs can have curves with steep or gentle slopes. They can include features such as the following:

- **Thresholds:** a minimum level of performance required before incentive payout begins (for example, 75% of quota)

- **Accelerators:** a higher rate of incentive payout as sales increase, designed to motivate top performance

- **Decelerators:** a lower rate of incentive payout as sales increase, designed to protect the company against windfalls

- **Caps:** a limit on the total amount of incentive money a salesperson can earn, designed to protect the company against windfalls

A good payout formula ensures a plan motivates the vast majority of salespeople, pays the right money to the right people (pays for performance) and is fiscally responsible. Chapter 8 provides examples of analytics you can use as part of a plan health check to help you track plan performance and assess whether your payout formula is achieving these objectives.

Combining Metrics and Payout Formulas for Incentive Plans That Drive Results

Effective incentive plan design requires combining metrics and payout formulas to create an incentive plan that fits your circumstances and encourages sales force activity aligned with your business objectives.

Incentive Plan Design Choices

Figure 3-5 provides several simplified examples of different incentive plans and describes the circumstances in which each is appropriate.

No incentive plan is perfect. Even if you choose the best plan for your circumstances, there will be issues you'll need to manage.

Commission plans that pay salespeople a percentage of all sales can create two issues. First, salespeople with above-average territory potential will have an easier time making money than salespeople in territories with few attractive accounts or tough competition. From a fairness perspective, commission plans that pay on all sales work best when market potential is equitably distributed across territories or when no single territory is close to tapping its potential, making differences across territories irrelevant. Such plans can also work in part-time direct sales forces, such as Avon and Amway, where the number of expected work hours and pay vary by salesperson.

Another issue with commission plans that pay for all sales is "hidden salary" for annuity or repeat sales. For example, at an industrial packaging company, two-thirds of the company's annual revenue was driven by multiyear contracts customers signed in prior years – these annuity or repeat sales occurred regardless of the effort salespeople put forth in the current year. Commissions paid on these sales were really a hidden salary; salespeople earned them almost automatically.

In environments with high repeat sales, companies paying commission from the first dollar sold often overestimate the extent to which pay is tied to current performance. The industrial packaging company thought its 75:25 pay mix gave salespeople strong incentives to sell. In fact, two-thirds of the 25% earned as incentive was hidden salary. The true guaranteed component of pay was more than 90%! Commission plans work best when they pay for sales resulting from effort salespeople put forth in the current year.

Quota-based plans can help to address both these issues. By giving each salesperson a quota and making incentive payout a function of quota attainment, quota-based plans can offer market-level earnings

Plan Description	Simplified Example	Appropriate Circumstances
Commission	Pay 5% of sales	• Launch and early-stage growth products • Hunter sales roles • Part-time direct sales forces (such as Avon and Amway)
Quota Based	$15,000 bonus at 90% of quota $25,000 bonus at 100% of quota $5,000 bonus for every 3% over quota	• Late-stage growth and mature products • Account management sales roles • Situations with many annuity or repeat sales • Situations with reasonably accurate territory sales forecasts
MBO	**MBO** / **% MBO Target Pay** Complete level 2 sales skills training — 20% Conduct 4 meetings with key decision makers — 30% Achieve distribution in 8 of top 10 accounts — 50%	• Situations in which individual results are not measurable • Customer-facing roles with limited sales impact • Local sales teams that need to tailor a portion of incentives to their specific situation • Sales activities before a product launch
Sales Ranking	Force-rank salespeople on sales volume: Top 10% gets $40,000 Next 20% gets $5,000 Next 20% gets $20,000 Bottom 10% gets $0 Next 40% gets $10,000	• Situations in which accurate sales forecasting is difficult • Situations requiring fiscal responsibility of a fixed payout • Sales forces that can manage the risk of unhealthy internal competition
Matrix	**Territory Sales (Millions)** | Price Discount	$2.3	$2.5	$2.7
15%	1.3	1.5	1.7
20%	0.9	1.1	1.3
25%	0.5	0.7	0.9 | Multiple of target pay Target pay = $25,000	• Situations with a need to balance multiple sales force priorities • Sales forces that can manage the complexity

Figure 3-5. Types of Sales Incentive Plans

opportunities to salespeople even if their territories have unequal market potential (provided each quota reflects the potential of the territory). Quota-based plans can also help minimize hidden salary by starting or accelerating payout at a threshold quota achievement level that challenges the salesperson to produce more than just annuity or repeat sales.

The key issue with quota-based plans is poor-quality quota setting. Such plans are effective only if quotas provide a reasonable but not unrealistic stretch and are fair across the sales force. Because quota setting is such a challenging issue, Chapter 9 is dedicated to the topic of setting fair and motivating quotas.

Linking Incentive Design to the Product Life Cycle

The framework shown in Figure 3-6 helps you choose metrics and payout formulas that match your business objectives and forecasting accuracy at different product life-cycle stages.

As an example of the framework, consider how a biotechnology company changed the incentive plan metrics and payout formula over a period surrounding the company's first product launch into a new and largely unknown market. The following changes reflected the evolution of the sales role, as well as the company's ability to forecast sales:

Several months leading up to launch. Salespeople focused on developing account plans and making initial sales calls to create awareness and identify decision makers.

Plan design: Incentives were linked to MBO achievement.

In the first year following launch. Salespeople focused on establishing relationships with key decision makers and generating early product sales. The company had moderate confidence in the national sales forecast but low confidence in territory-level sales forecasts.

Plan design: Incentives were linked to sales, paid as a commission on total territory sales, with a small added bonus if the national sales quota was achieved.

In the following year. Salespeople focused on driving territory sales growth by realizing more opportunities with existing customers and developing new customers. The company had high confidence in the national sales forecast and moderately high confidence in territory-level sales forecasts.

Plan design: Incentives were linked to territory sales quota attainment, with payout starting at 75% of quota and accelerating beyond 100%.

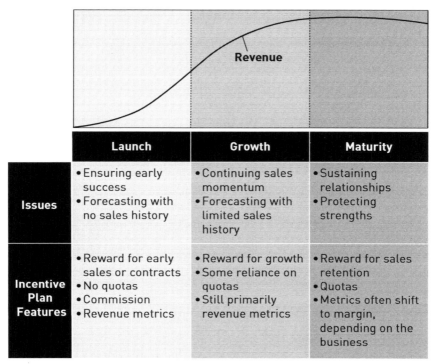

	Launch	Growth	Maturity
Issues	• Ensuring early success • Forecasting with no sales history	• Continuing sales momentum • Forecasting with limited sales history	• Sustaining relationships • Protecting strengths
Incentive Plan Features	• Reward for early sales or contracts • No quotas • Commission • Revenue metrics	• Reward for growth • Some reliance on quotas • Still primarily revenue metrics	• Reward for sales retention • Quotas • Metrics often shift to margin, depending on the business

Figure 3-6. Typical Choices for Incentive Compensation Plan Design Across the Product Life Cycle

Conclusion

Four key sales compensation design decisions can help you create the right plan for driving sales force performance. The first two decisions – pay level and pay mix – set the sales compensation plan structure. The next two decisions – metrics and payout formula – focus on designing the incentive portion of pay. Subsequent chapters of this book discuss how these decisions can help you address the key issues you may be struggling with today, such as changing sales roles, workforce diversity, company profitability and global effectiveness. The right sales compensation design is an important component of any solution for tackling these and other issues and for positioning your sales force for future success.

Endnotes

1   Ashutosh Muduli and Vinita Kaura, "Southwest Airlines Success: A Case Study Analysis," *BVIMR Management Edge* 4, no. 2 (2011): 115–18.

2   ZS Incentive Practices Research (IPR) study. Data are gathered annually through a survey of sales compensation professionals in multiple industries worldwide. Results are provided to participating companies.

3   Andris A. Zoltners, Prabhakant Sinha and Sally E. Lorimer, *The Complete Guide to Sales Force Incentive Compensation: How to Design and Implement Plans That Work* (New York: AMACOM, 2006).

SECTION 2

Addressing Recent Sales Compensation Issues

The next five chapters focus on sales compensation challenges brought about by changes in today's business environment. These chapters share actionable ideas for addressing recent issues.

Chapter 4   Aligning Compensation With Changing Sales Roles

Learn how sales roles are adapting to the needs of better-informed customers in the digital world and the implications for sales compensation.

Chapter 5   Motivating the Sales Force With More Than Money

Align your compensation plan with a broader sales force motivation program that appeals to the diverse motivational needs of salespeople.

Chapter 6   Driving Profit, Not Just Sales

Design sales compensation plans and metrics to encourage the sales force to deliver *profitable* sales growth.

Chapter 7   Going Global With Sales Compensation

Create global consistency in sales compensation without losing the flexibility to meet local country needs.

Chapter 8   Using Analytics to Boost Sales Compensation Impact

Use information technology, digital channels and analytics to improve sales compensation plan performance.

CHAPTER 4

Aligning Compensation With Changing Sales Roles

A Changing World of Corporate Buying

Joe, a corporate buyer of computer products, had just finished placing a large order for new laptop computers for the global consulting firm he worked for. This would be the first of several orders required to complete a major technology upgrade for the firm.

Planning for the laptop upgrade had been in the works for many months. After doing an assessment of the needs of consultants at the firm, Joe started educating himself about product alternatives and prices. He gathered information about different laptops from the websites of the firm's preferred computer resellers and looked at independent online sources, such as articles, reviews and white papers. He also tapped into social media to learn about the experiences of other customers with different products. This initial research gave him a good base of knowledge as a starting point.

Joe's next step was to contact an account manager, Lisa, from the reseller Joe selected to work with. Joe had been working with Lisa for many years, and she understood the firm's business needs. Joe trusted her to help him sift through all the information and misinformation he had gathered in his initial research. Lisa worked with Joe over email and the telephone and arranged videoconference meetings as needed to connect Joe and others at his firm with sales specialists and other experts who could help with the decision.

When Joe was ready to place an order, he used a customized web-based purchasing portal provided by the reseller. He liked the convenience of self-service order placement and the portal's easy-to-use features for managing and tracking shipping and keeping on top of the firm's hardware and software license inventories.

Joe felt a sense of accomplishment as he clicked the "place order" button. He reflected on how much the buying process had changed since he had started his career in the early 1990s. Back then, he had relied on account managers from the computer manufacturers, such as IBM and Dell, as his key source of information and support when buying. These salespeople would knock down his door to get a face-to-face meeting so they could share product information, demonstrate the latest technology and place orders for him. In the early 2000s when the manufacturers began to sell through resellers, Joe got much of his product information from a reseller's hard copy catalog, with occasional live meetings with the reseller's account manager. Often, he would talk to a reseller's inside salesperson over the telephone to ask questions and place orders.

Today, Joe did most purchasing online by using the customized, self-service purchasing portals the resellers provided. Usually, there was no need to involve an account manager. Most purchases were familiar products and repeat orders for which Joe knew exactly what he needed. If he had a question that wasn't addressed on the website, it was convenient to contact an online chat representative for an answer. Still, Joe was glad he had maintained relationships with Lisa and a few other trusted account managers at the resellers. With the major technology upgrade the firm now faced, Lisa had really helped him make the right decisions and navigate the complex implementation process.

How Sales Roles Are Changing

Joe's experience illustrates the transformation in buying and selling that has occurred in many business markets in recent decades. Buyers, enabled by the internet, have become more informed and self-sufficient. Selling companies are using more efficient sales channels to reach these customers and are adapting their sales roles to fundamental changes in what customers need and expect from salespeople. The role of the field salesperson as purveyor of information and order taker has largely disappeared. Some companies and industries are affected by these dynamics more than others, but almost all are feeling some impact, and that impact is increasing.

However, this shift to customer self-service and use of non-field sales channels hasn't eliminated the role of the field salesperson completely. In fact, salespeople are still an important influence in many customer buying situations. The key for selling companies is to identify situations in which salespeople can create unique value for customers and to refocus the role of the field salesperson accordingly. This means redefining field sales roles to focus on two priorities:

1. helping customers who need help, often with complex and uncertain buying decisions

2. orchestrating an efficient customer buying process across multiple channels

This chapter explores how companies are adapting field sales roles to emphasize these priorities and the impact of this sales role change on sales compensation.

Focusing on Customers Who Need Help

When leaders at Dow Corning observed in the early 2000s that some customers wanted an easier, more affordable way to buy the company's standard silicone products, they created XIAMETER® a brand that included thousands of products that were less differentiated – approximately 30% of the products Dow Corning sold.[1] Self-sufficient customers could buy XIAMETER products without the help of a salesperson through a low-cost, no-frills, self-service online sales channel. Customers who desired a higher-touch approach could still purchase products from a salesperson under the Dow Corning brand name, which also included specialty silicones backed by research and technical services. Customers could choose how they wanted to buy and could use different channels for different purchases, depending on their needs.

For years, selling companies have been tailoring sales roles to the needs of different customer segments. A common approach is to look at customer potential and to create three sales roles:

1. a key account role to serve the needs of high-potential customers

2. a field sales role to cover midmarket customers

3. an inside sales role to serve low-potential customers

Companies have also traditionally assigned sales roles on the basis of product and service needs. For example, a technical sales specialist is assigned to help a customer design and implement a complex, customized solution.

Today many companies are discovering these traditional criteria for segmenting customers are insufficient. Customer knowledge and self-sufficiency are growing drivers of how customers want to buy and, thus, are key determinants of the sales roles required to reach different customers at different times. Some customers are self-service and want to buy on their own; others are information seeking and want help from salespeople. For any single customer, the buying preference can vary from purchase to purchase, and often a customer's desired approach falls in between the two extremes – for example, a customer wants to purchase online but wants help from a salesperson over click-to-chat.

Multiple sales roles are required to serve the needs of different customer segments and at different times. Each sales role needs a compensation plan that attracts the right candidates and motivates the right sales activities for that role.

Orchestrating the Customer Connection

In the pharmaceutical industry, physician education once occurred mostly through face-to-face contact between salespeople and physicians. That is no longer the case today. Instead, companies are tracking individual physician communication preferences and reaching out with the combination of face-to-face visits and digital methods (which include customized mobile apps and podcasts) that best meets each physician's needs. Salespeople visit physicians who like to get information through face-to-face interaction, and they also play a role in coordinating communication with physicians who prefer multiple digital channels.

In many industries, sales process responsibility is increasingly shared by salespeople and digital communication channels. Salespeople can help to coordinate the multichannel outreach to customers by taking on a role as orchestrators who ensure buyers get a consistent and well-timed message. As buyers become more comfortable collaborating with salespeople remotely, field salespeople, in addition to visiting customers in person, also communicate via email, telephone and videoconferencing. Field salespeople also may coordinate with inside salespeople who share responsibility for their customers. For key customers who seek help from salespeople as consultants, the task of orchestration can become very complex. Besides coordination of multiple communication channels and inside and field sales outreach, the orchestration for these customers can involve teams of sales specialists or experts from other company departments, such as logistics or finance.

As sales processes use more sales roles and digital channels, sales compensation plans must adapt to encourage orchestration of the right sales activities and channels for meeting customer needs, while rewarding salespeople appropriately for their contribution to sales outcomes.

Adapting Compensation to Changing Sales Roles

As companies redefine the role of many salespeople in response to these dynamics, existing sales compensation plans can become misaligned with the new sales role responsibilities and expectations. Current compensation plans may not attract and retain the right salespeople for new roles. In addition, current plans may not motivate and direct salespeople to engage in the right sales activity to meet customer needs and may fail to pay for performance.

Companies must modify sales compensation plans to align with sales role changes. Often, they must implement other sales force changes as well, including modifications to sales processes, sales force size and structure, hiring and coaching, sales tools and information, and performance management.

The remainder of this chapter focuses on how companies can adapt their sales compensation plans to reinforce today's changing sales roles. Many companies are just starting to explore how sales compensation decisions such as pay level, pay mix and metrics are affected.

Aligning Pay Levels With the Value of Today's Sales Roles

As sales role change affects the skills salespeople need to succeed, as well as the impact salespeople have with customers, companies must re-evaluate the benchmarks they use for setting sales force pay levels. The impact on pay level varies by customer segment.

Companies typically need fewer field salespeople to meet the needs of knowledgeable and self-sufficient customers. At the same time, they can often serve these customers with salespeople in less expensive roles.

For example, when purchasing a printer, a self-sufficient customer may already know the specifications she needs and the maximum price she is willing to pay. She may search the company's website for a printer with the desired specifications. If she can't find exactly what she's looking for, she may click on a link that says, "Would you like to chat with a representative?" The representative helps the customer by sending her a link to a product that meets her needs and then walking her through the online order process.

Compare this with the sales role required to help an information-seeking customer buy a printer. The customer needs help with figuring out what model and features he needs. He talks with a salesperson at length about how he will use the printer. The salesperson listens, figures out what model and features to recommend and then demonstrates several options for the customer. After closing the sale and completing the purchase, the salesperson connects the customer with resources for getting post-purchase technical support.

The pay level for the representative helping the self-sufficient customer is likely lower than the pay level for the salesperson helping the information-seeking customer for two reasons. First, the skills required to serve the self-sufficient customer have less value in the labor market. These include skills in understanding product features and answering customers' questions about production specifications. Many people have these skills, sometimes in countries with low-cost labor markets.

The skills required to help the information-seeking customer have higher value in the labor market. These include skills in consulting and problem solving and perhaps orchestrating with other people and communication channels to address a customer's needs. Fewer people have these skills; attracting and keeping salespeople for such roles requires higher total pay.

Second, the representative who helped the self-sufficient customer likely gets lower incentive pay because the representative's impact on the sale is less compared with that of the salesperson who helped the information-seeking customer. The representative had some impact; without help, the self-sufficient customer might not have found the right printer and might have jumped to another company's website. However, the representative's impact is not as great as that of the salesperson who had to assist the information-seeking customer throughout all steps of the buying process.

Chapter 3 provides more information about pay level decisions and how salespeople's skills and impact influence pay level.

Aligning Pay Mix and Metrics With Today's Sales Roles

In many industries and companies today, sales process execution involves multiple sales roles and channels. When a salesperson helps with a sale to a knowledgeable or self-sufficient customer, the salesperson likely shares influence on the sale with digital channels that also influenced the customer – for example, social media, information on the company's website and the company's online ordering and post-sales support systems. When a salesperson helps with a sale to an information-seeking customer, the salesperson's influence on the buying decision is likely greater. However, that influence is often shared with digital channels and other sales team members, such as technical or financing specialists and inside salespeople.

In either case, a single salesperson has only partial influence on the sale, and the impact of that individual is difficult to isolate and measure. At the same time, success in this environment requires multiple channels and sales team members to function cohesively together to meet customer needs and drive sales.

Rethinking Pay Mix

One way to adjust sales compensation to reflect the reduction in individual salesperson influence and performance measurability, while encouraging a cohesive sales approach for customers, is to reduce the incentive portion of pay.

Incentives are most effective when a single salesperson's knowledge, skills and activities are the key influence on a customer's buying decision and when there are measurable performance metrics. When sales process responsibility is shared by multiple channels and salespeople, it becomes difficult to isolate and measure the influence of individual salespeople. Thus, it can make sense to reduce sales force incentives, pay salespeople a larger salary with a reasonable bonus and use programs other than short-term cash incentives to motivate and direct salespeople. These other programs can include performance management, coaching and training, sales force data and tools, a different hiring profile and other sales force programs. All these programs can be more powerful than incentives for setting the right tone for the sales force, affecting sales force behavior and enhancing performance. To implement these programs, the company and its sales managers must take a more active role in managing and motivating the sales team.

Reducing the incentive portion of pay is a difficult change for many sales forces. A large variable component of pay can drive business success. After all, many executives receive stock options as part of their compensation, so they have a vested interest in making the company stronger, more competitive and more prosperous in the long run. Incentives help to keep sales force costs in line with revenues, and they are an important part of the culture in many sales forces – a culture that pays for performance, motivates salespeople to reach and exceed company goals and attracts and retains high achievers for sales roles. Drastic changes to this culture could disrupt and alienate salespeople and hurt sales. There could also be a first-mover disadvantage in that salespeople who are currently producing high levels of sales might leave a company that reduces incentive pay to join one that still provides a significant upside earnings opportunity.

The arguments for and against reducing the incentive portion of pay in today's environment are summarized in Figure 4-1.

Rethinking Performance Metrics

An alternative to modifying the pay mix is to acknowledge changes in individual salesperson influence and performance measurability by changing the metrics that determine incentive pay. Most traditional sales incentive plans focus on short-term, individual results metrics (for example, quarterly territory sales). By linking sales force pay to more team-based, longer-term and activity-based metrics, companies can encourage the team-oriented and multichannel sales approach required for long-term success with customers. Effectively, this makes sales incentive plans look more like management bonus plans. However, this approach creates some challenges that need to be managed.

First, team-based incentive plans can sometimes attract security-minded people rather than the go-getters likely to become superstar salespeople. Team-based plans can sometimes create a free-rider problem in which a few non-performing members of a team benefit from the actions of the productive members. If not managed effectively, star performers may subsidize poor performers. Some companies seek to address this problem by using formulas to share sales credit among

Arguments FOR Reducing the Incentive Portion of Pay
In an environment of shared sales process responsibility: • It is difficult to isolate and measure the influence of individual salespeople on short-term results. • Individual incentives are less effective. **Other sales force programs (coaching, performance management, sales data and tools) may work better than incentives for:** • setting the right tone • affecting sales force behavior • enhancing performance

Arguments AGAINST Reducing the Incentive Portion of Pay
Despite shared sales responsibility, incentives still: • give salespeople a vested interest in making the company successful • motivate salespeople and attract high achievers • help keep sales force costs in line with revenues • increase peer pressure to perform **Reducing incentive pay is risky because of the following factors:** • It can disrupt and alienate salespeople and hurt sales. • There may be a first-mover disadvantage. Salespeople producing high levels of current sales may leave to join another company that still offers greater incentive opportunity.

Figure 4-1. Arguments For and Against Reducing the Incentive Portion of Sales Force Pay

different team members, but too often, such formulas are complex and it's difficult to get agreement on them. If formulas change frequently, plan administration becomes difficult. If salespeople don't fully understand or agree with the formulas, the power of the incentive to motivate is diminished.

Paying for longer-term performance creates challenges as well. Incentives have the most impact when the reward is received soon after the work gets done. The motivational power of an incentive paid out annually, for example, is likely less than that of an incentive paid soon after a big sale is realized. Companies can supplement plans paying for longer-term performance by making more frequent payments tied to the achievement of intermediate milestones; the challenge is how best to track and measure progress.

With team-based and long-term incentives, sales managers must play a role in knowing who the stars are and in making sure they get appropriately recognized and rewarded in a timely fashion. Also, motivators other than money become more important for keeping the sales force continually engaged.

Another approach to performance metrics for today's sales roles is to focus on sales force activities instead of results. Shared sales process responsibility makes it difficult to determine who caused the results, but incentives can help ensure the activities contributing to the results get done. Salespeople might be evaluated not on what they sell but on how they coordinate and bring value to their customers and, therefore, contribute to a sale. In one case, success may be sharing product knowledge with a customer. In another, success may involve bringing in a specialist. The idea is to reward salespeople for effectively performing the activities required for successful selling.

Challenges exist when paying salespeople for activities. First, investors reward the company for results, not activity. Second, it is difficult to measure activity accurately. Salespeople may misstate what they actually do. Finally, tracking activity can motivate an increase in the *quantity* of the desired activity but a decrease in the *quality*. Often, activity measurement works best when it's used as part of the performance management process but not as a determinant of incentive pay. This helps to build a sales culture in which salespeople choose to engage in the right activities for driving success with customers rather than a "vending machine" culture in which salespeople expect payment for their actions.

The arguments for and against changing the performance metrics for today's environment are summarized in Figure 4-2. Chapter 3 includes more information about what factors to consider when determining sales force pay mix and performance metrics.

Conclusion

Today's sales roles are evolving, and companies are in the early stages of figuring out what the implications are for sales compensation. The speed at which change is occurring and the degree of impact vary across industries and companies. What is certain is that change is necessary, and implementing it will not be easy. As sales roles evolve, sales compensation must align with the new responsibilities and expectations for salespeople. Some of the changes that may be required (for example, a pay mix with a smaller individual incentive component, new performance metrics that potentially redistribute income among salespeople, possible

Arguments FOR New Performance Metrics (Why to De-Emphasize Individual, Short-Term, and Results Metrics)

In an environment of shared sales process responsibility:
- It is difficult to isolate and measure the influence of individual salespeople on short-term results.

Incentives tied to team-based, long-term or activity metrics may work better for:
- setting the right tone
- affecting sales force behavior
- enhancing long-term performance

Arguments AGAINST New Performance Metrics (Why to Keep the Focus on Individual, Short-Term, and Results Metrics)

Team-based incentives can attract security-minded people and can unfairly reward free riders.

Long-term incentives may have less impact because the reward is received long after the work gets done.

Activity-based incentives create measurement challenges and can reinforce an inappropriate "vending machine" culture.

Figure 4-2. Arguments For and Against New Incentive Plan Performance Metrics

pay reductions for some roles) are difficult to implement without sales force and customer disruption.

Because of the numerous implementation challenges, at many companies, sales compensation plan change is likely to lag sales role change, but there is a considerable downside to waiting too long to adapt sales compensation for new sales roles. Companies may experience higher-than-necessary sales compensation costs, insufficient attraction and retention of the right kind of talent and a failure to motivate the right sales activities for meeting the needs of today's customers.

Companies that make evolutionary improvements to sales compensation on a regular basis are better positioned to adapt to the changing environment without significant interruption to their business. However, transformational change is sometimes necessary in cases in which customer and company results are seriously threatened or when dramatic environmental change is occurring.

Chapter 10 shares ideas and strategies for what to do to gain sales force acceptance when salespeople resist sales compensation change.

Endnote

1   Bob Frei and Chris Musso, "Innovation in Chemicals: An Interview With Dow Corning's Stephanie Burns and Gregg Zank," *McKinsey on Chemicals*, Winter 2011, 22–27.

CHAPTER 5

Motivating the Sales Force With More Than Money

Addressing Sales Force Diversity and Motivation

Energizing a sales force would be much easier if all salespeople were motivated by identical things. But of course they aren't. People have various capabilities, experiences and financial needs. They are born in different generations and are at different stages of their careers. They have various work, cultural and educational backgrounds, and they have different personalities and tolerance for risk. All of these factors can affect motivation.

The entry of a large number of Millennial generation workers into sales forces has created different diversity in what motivates and engages salespeople. Addressing this diversity requires creativity in designing sales compensation plans. It also requires thinking beyond cash incentives to design broader motivation programs that engage salespeople who have different wants and needs. *Motivation is about more than incentives.* In fact, practically every sales force decision influences motivation to some degree. At the same time, *incentives are about more than motivation.* They also help to align salespeople's activities with company strategies and keep sales force costs in line with results. Motivating a diverse sales force requires careful attention to the motivational aspects of compensation plans, as well as investment in other programs that use rewards other than money to energize salespeople.

This chapter is organized around the following three steps for developing a broad sales force motivation program for engaging a diverse sales force:

1. understanding human motivation

2. determining the dominant motivational profiles in your sales force

3. designing a varied motivational program, including a sales compensation plan, that appeals to all of the dominant motivational profiles

Generational Diversity: Motivating the Millennials

The issue of motivating a diverse sales force has become particularly salient in the last decade as the Millennials (people in their 20s to mid-30s in 2017) have entered the workforce. Millennials have a lot to say about what it's like to work with older sales force members:

- "I feel underappreciated by my 40-something-year-old [Generation X] sales manager. I'm ready to take on more varied and interesting assignments. At least, I deserve more appreciation for my work. My parents agree with me that the company is underutilizing my talents."

- "Our 60-something-year-old [Baby Boomer] VP of Sales sends out lengthy emails. She calls and leaves voicemail messages when a quick text would be much easier to respond to. She is knowledgeable, but it's more efficient for me to get information using the internet or by reaching out to my network on social media."

- "As a 28-year-old new manager, one of my biggest challenges is a 50-something-year-old [Baby Boomer] salesperson on my team. He works hard but won't respond to texts sent after his workday is done. That's frustrating for me because I occasionally leave the job before 5 p.m. to go to the gym and like to catch up on work in the evening."

Generational differences are a big source of diversity in most sales forces. Throughout this chapter, examples of generational diversity are used to illustrate how motivation programs that provide something for every generation in your sales force can drive broader engagement.

Understanding Human Motivation

Understanding the complexities of what motivates different individuals is a first step in developing a sales force motivation program.

Five Universal Motivators of Salespeople

There is a good deal of research aimed at explaining what motivates people. Theories of motivation focus on understanding the needs of individuals and their drive to fill those needs. Maslow's hierarchy of needs is an example of a classic motivation theory. Maslow's hierarchy is often illustrated as a pyramid with more basic physiological needs at the bottom and higher-level self-actualization needs at the top.

The framework shown in Figure 5-1 draws on Maslow's and others' motivation theories to suggest five universal motivators relevant for sales forces. All salespeople share these universal motivators to some extent, but the importance of each varies by person. Motivating the sales force requires offering programs that fulfill all five of these universal needs.

Individual Differences

Motivation theory provides insights about why individuals behave in a particular way and how individuals are different. Consider, for example, five salespeople from one sales force:

Ann, ranked 4th of 100 in the nation

- Ignores the company-assigned quota and sets goals for herself that are much higher
- Has been on the big incentive trip every year since joining the company
- Talks to her manager only if there is a concern about the sales tools
- Regularly reads blogs on selling tips and strategies

Beth, ranked 48th of 100 in the nation

- Usually makes quota but was sweating it out until the fourth quarter last year
- Loves to play golf and seems to know people everywhere she goes
- Has more than 1,000 connections on LinkedIn
- Loves sharing ideas and kudos on the internal sales force message board

Need	Examples of What Companies Can Offer to Satisfy This Need
Achievement: To feel "I'm succeeding."	• Measurement of and frequent feedback on performance • Challenging but achievable goals or quotas • Incentive plans that pay for performance • Sales contests and Special Performance Incentives for Field Force (SPIFFs) • Autonomy and personal responsibility • Opportunities to grow and solve new problems • Challenging and meaningful work
Social Affiliation: To feel "People like me."	• Friendly coworkers, managers and customers • In-person sales meetings, training and best practice sharing • Trips and conferences • Cooperative, non-competitive team-oriented situations • Social networking intranet sites
Power: To feel "I run things."	• Empowerment through information and training (don't micromanage) • Promotions and leadership roles • Competitive and status-oriented situations • Participation in decision making
Ego Gratification: To feel "I'm the best."	• Promotions and special titles • Plaques and recognition (for example, President's Club) • Money, cars, tech gadgets, a gold watch • Praise from the boss
Survival: To feel "I won't fail."	• Job security • Training, coaching and information support

Figure 5-1. Five Universal Motivators of Salespeople[1]

Cathy, ranked 58th of 100 in the nation

- Usually makes quota but at any point in the year might be far ahead or behind
- Resists her manager's offers for extra assistance on difficult sales calls
- Liked the last sales meeting but complained that the salespeople did not have any input about the meeting's location
- Uses the internal sales force website to stay informed; rarely stops by the regional office

Donna, ranked 10th of 100 in the nation

- Takes reaching quota as a given and is much more concerned with her ranking
- Loves compliments on her performance
- Has a wall in her home office displaying all her sales awards
- Was thrilled to be the featured star last month in the internal sales force e-newsletter

Ellen, ranked 91st of 100 in the nation

- Is not making quota in her second year and her future in sales is uncertain
- Likes her manager's coaching but is worried about the performance warnings
- Tells her manager that sales meetings take up too much of her customer selling time

Each of these five salespeople is motivated primarily by a different universal motivator:

1. **Ann** is motivated mostly by *achievement.* Her desire for success gets her through the tough times.
2. **Beth** is motivated mostly by *social affiliation.* She enjoys being part of the group, and her social skills go a long way in sales.
3. **Cathy** is motivated mostly by *power.* She wants to control her own life, and a sales job allows her to do that as long as she delivers.
4. **Donna** is motivated mostly by *ego gratification.* She wants to be the best, and her ego keeps her bouncing back after every rejection from a prospect.
5. **Ellen** is motivated mostly by *survival.* She's working hard to make it in the company.

Provided Ann, Beth, Cathy, Donna and Ellen have the capabilities needed for the sales job, all of them have the potential to be successful. The secret is finding the right way to motivate each individual. This requires a varied motivational program with something that can appeal to each of the five universal motivators.

Determining the Dominant Motivational Profiles of Your Sales Force

In order to use motivation theory to help design a sales force motivation program, you need to segment your salespeople according to their motivational profiles. By understanding differences across segments, you can determine what incentives and other motivation programs you'll need to appeal to every segment.

One way to segment salespeople is to use demographic characteristics as an indicator of motivational needs. For example, people of the same generation or career stage are likely to be motivated by similar things. Another way to segment is to assess the motivational needs of each member of your sales force directly – for example, to measure the extent to which individuals are motivated by achievement, social affiliation, power, ego gratification and survival – and to segment based on the assessment results. These two approaches are described here.

Segmentation by Demographic Characteristics

Demographic characteristics, such as career stage, gender, culture and educational background, can be good indicators of what is likely to motivate different sales force members. A popular approach involves segmenting by generation.

Sociologists theorize that the unique historical and cultural events that members of each generation experience affect what is important to them and thus affect their approach to work.

In today's workforce, three generations are most relevant – Baby Boomers, Generation Xers and Millennials (sometimes referred to as "Generation Y"). Figure 5-2 summarizes the approximate age range for each generation and some typical differences reflected in the majority of research regarding what shaped each generation, what each generation desires and needs, and what companies can offer to satisfy these wants and needs.

Generations and What Shaped Them	What Is Desired and Needed	Examples of What Companies Can Offer to Satisfy These Wants and Needs
Baby Boomers Born 1946–1964, 29% of 2015 workforce[3] *Shaped by:* Vietnam; Cold War; moon landing; JFK, RFK, MLK assassinations; civil rights, women's movements; TV; rock and roll	• Professional identity • Material wealth • Competition • Respect for hard work • In-office face time	• Recognition of success • Pay increases • Opportunity to make a difference
Generation X Born 1965–1980, 34% of 2015 workforce[3] *Shaped by:* Working parents (latchkey kids), Gulf War, *Challenger* explosion, AIDS, corporate downsizing, video games	• Mobility and autonomy • Work-life balance • Being your own person	• Empowerment • Opportunity for promotion • Flexible work schedule • Time off
Millennials Born 1981–1997, 34% of 2015 workforce[3] *Shaped by:* Involved, nurturing parents; 9/11 and terrorism; cell phones, text messaging and social networking; cooperative learning at school	• Praise and encouragement • Meaningful and socially responsible work • Connection through technology • Opportunity to work with diverse teams	• Frequent coaching, feedback and promotions • Opportunity to see the big picture • Time off to volunteer • Latest mobile devices with fun, visual feedback • Recognition and rewards for teamwork

Figure 5-2. Generations in the Workforce and What Is Important for Motivating Salespeople[2,3,4,5]

Too often, motivation programs are designed by people of a specific generation and, thus, appeal to other people of the same generation (for example, boomers design programs that appeal to other boomers). An effective motivational program acknowledges generational diversity. A breakdown of your sales force across generations can provide insight about the best way to structure a program.

Generational Diversity: Motivating Millennial Salespeople

Although the research about what motivates Millennials is not totally consistent, most researchers agree that several unique life experiences of Millennials have shaped this generation.

Nurturing Parents. Millennials were raised by helicopter parents who gave them constant attention and validation. They were recognized with trophies for every success.

Implications for how to motivate: Give repeated feedback and reassurance – a formal annual performance review isn't enough. Provide access to up-to-the-minute feedback on performance by using technology that is fun, visual and entertaining. Provide frequent opportunity for promotion.

Digital Natives. Millennials grew up in a world of cell phones, text messaging and social networks. They are great at multitasking and see no point to being in the office during standard hours if someone can text them when they are needed.

Implications for how to motivate: Arm them with the latest mobile devices and apps to help them do their job better.

Some Unique Life-Changing Events. Millennials were influenced by unprecedented terrorism and school violence during their formative years, so they know that bad things can happen to anyone anytime. As a result, they will question whether or not their work is meaningful and want to make a positive contribution to society quickly.

Implications for how to motivate: Show them how their work fits into the bigger picture; give them time off to volunteer.

Cooperative Learning. Education for Millennials involved cooperative learning and team projects, so they believe that teamwork trumps individual effort and that ideas should come from everyone, regardless of their job title.

Implications for how to motivate: Create opportunities for team building and socializing; recognize and reward for teamwork.

Segmentation by Motivational Needs

Although it's relatively easy to segment your sales force using demographic characteristics, such as generation, it's not always accurate to assume that everyone in the same age group is motivated in the same way. If people within a generation in a sales force are motivated by different things, then it's important to look beyond demographic characteristics when designing a motivation program.

An alternative way to segment a sales force for purposes of understanding motivation is to measure salespeople's motivational needs directly by using an assessment tool. Such tools or tests ask individuals to make choices that reveal their motivational needs within a specific framework (for example, the framework of Five Universal Motivators of Salespeople shown in Figure 5-1). On the basis of the assessment results, you can identify segments of salespeople who have common motivational needs and tailor motivation programs to the needs of each segment.

Assessment tools are built around different motivational frameworks. For example, a sales force from a large pharmaceutical and medical device company used a modified version of a framework popularized by Harvard Business School professors Paul Lawrence and Nitin Nohria[6] to assess the motivational needs of its salespeople.

The company had two sales roles participating in the same sales incentive structure:

- **Account sales specialists** spent their time selling new business. These sales-focused professionals generally had considerable sales experience and a longer tenure with the company. Account sales specialists earned incentives of $300 per device sold.

- **Relationship specialists** performed a customer support role. Most had backgrounds in the healthcare field (many were former nurses) and a shorter tenure with the company. Each relationship specialist was teamed with three account sales specialists and earned sales incentives of $100 per device sold.

The company tested individuals in both the account sales and the relationship specialist roles to see which of four inherent drives from Lawrence and Nohria's framework dominated:

1. **Acquire:** the need to obtain things that provide a sense of well-being and improve social status

2. **Bond:** the need to connect with others in the family, organization and community

3. **Learn:** the need to understand and grow

4. **Defend:** the need to defend properties and relationships, rooted in the basic fight-or-flight response

By using a conjoint statistical technique, the company analyzed people's choices on the test and discovered that the importance of each drive varied across the two groups:

- **Account sales specialists** were motivated 85% by the drive to **acquire**.

- **Relationship specialists** were motivated more equally by the drive to **acquire** and the drive to **bond**.

With this discovery, the company questioned whether it was appropriate to have both roles participate in the same basic incentive plan structure. The current plan appealed to the acquire drive and, thus, was motivating for account sales specialists. However, relationship specialists might find an alternative plan more motivating if it offered opportunities to participate in educational programs, conferences and other social and team-building events, along with a smaller cash incentive.

Designing a Varied Motivational Program

With a good understanding of the dominant motivational profiles in your sales force, you can develop a motivational program that matches those profiles and keeps the entire sales force engaged. A good program has something for every major segment of your sales force.

The variety required in your motivational program depends on the diversity of your salespeople. A sales force that has equal numbers of Millennials, Gen Xers and Baby Boomers, for example, will require a more varied program than a sales force in which the vast majority of salespeople are of one generation. Another example draws on the Five Universal Motivators of Salespeople framework (see Figure 5-1). A sales force in which 50% of the people value achievement most and 50% value social affiliation most will require a more varied program than a sales force in which 90% value achievement most.

Typically, the cash sales incentive compensation plan is the core of a sales force motivation program. The core plan is supplemented by other programs (career paths, sales contests, Special Performance Incentives for Field Force [SPIFFs], recognition programs, sales meetings and events) that have motivation as a primary objective. In addition, many aspects of the company and sales force environment and culture can also affect motivation.

Core Sales Incentive Compensation Plan

There is general agreement that cash incentive compensation affects motivation by appealing to the achievement, ego-gratification and survival motivators in salespeople.

Making Key Incentive Plan Design Decisions

Regardless of the motivational profiles of the people in your sales force, each of the four key incentive plan design decisions can affect the power of incentives to motivate:

1. **Pay level:** Money serves as a success measure for salespeople and, thus, appeals to the achievement and ego-drive motivators. Also, the survival motive kicks in when there is fear of low pay.

2. **Pay mix:** A large incentive component is motivating to achievement-minded and ego-driven salespeople. The salary or guaranteed portion of pay should be large enough to provide sustenance pay to meet the need for survival.

3. **Metrics:** Results-based metrics (sales, growth, profits) appeal to salespeople's need for achievement and ego gratification.

4. **Plan type and payout formula:** Commission plans appeal to salespeople's achievement and ego-gratification needs. Quota-based plans also appeal to these needs, provided the quotas are challenging yet achievable. Payout formulas should invoke the achievement motivator in the vast majority of salespeople. Thresholds (minimums before payout starts) should ensure that only the lowest performers earn nothing. Accelerators (increases in payout rates as sales increase) should challenge top performers to earn the highest pay. Caps (limits on earnings) are generally demotivating and should be used only when necessary to protect the company against windfalls.

Customizing Your Incentive Plan for Individuals

An argument can be made that to maximize motivation across a diverse sales force you should customize sales incentive compensation plans for each individual. In the extreme, this would allow every salesperson to choose the pay level and mix, metrics, and plan type and payout formula that he or she finds most motivating. For example, salespeople with a high need for achievement could choose a plan with a high target pay level and a large at-risk incentive component linked to sales results. Those with a high need for survival and social affiliation might choose a plan with a lower target pay level and large guaranteed salary component, plus benefits outside of the core cash sales incentive compensation plan, such as attendance at educational programs and conferences.

From a practical standpoint, incentive plan customization would require addressing some big administrative and technical implementation challenges. The increased complexity of managing multiple plans could lead to overall incentive costs that are higher than with a single plan.

In addition, it could be necessary to manage the social comparison that could occur across the sales force. People might see their colleagues making more money, enjoying different perks, or doing both. They may feel remorse about picking the wrong plan. When considering whether to customize incentive plans, companies must develop strategies for managing these costs. More information about approaches for allowing salespeople to "pick their own plan" is available in *The Future of Sales Compensation* (Albrecht and Marley).[7]

Supplemental Motivation Program Components

In addition to the core incentive compensation plan, companies use several types of programs that are specifically designed to enhance sales force motivation. The key is to select a combination of programs that is well matched to the dominant motivational profiles of your sales force.

Career Paths

An established career track is an important motivational tool. Promotions appeal to the ego-gratification and achievement motivators by providing another way to win. Promotions also appeal to the power motivator by giving people the possibility of greater influence over decision making.

Many companies offer dual career paths. For example, a promotion to regional sales manager might appeal to the ego, achievement and power motivators of a salesperson with managerial desire and potential. An analogous promotion to strategic account manager could appeal to these motivators in a salesperson who is more valuable as an individual contributor.

Generational Diversity and Career Paths

The opportunity for promotion is especially important to Millennials who crave frequent and ongoing affirmation of their progress. Many Millennials are impatient; they don't want to wait three years for a promotion. In response, some companies have created more levels, shortened the performance management cycle or eliminated traditional performance management processes in favor of more frequent coaching.

Gen Xers, many of whom are in the establishment phase of their careers, also find the opportunity for career advancement to be a significant motivator. Career tracks that involve flexible work schedules can motivate individuals who have young families or Baby Boomers who are nearing retirement. Baby Boomers might also covet roles that allow them to share their experience with younger workers.

Contests and SPIFFs

Contests and SPIFFs are a powerful and relatively inexpensive way to energize salespeople and focus sales force attention on specific short-term goals. The terms "SPIFF" and "contest" are sometimes used interchangeably, but a key distinction is that SPIFFs usually allow many sales force members to earn money or prizes, and contests have salespeople compete with one another for a limited number of prizes. Both contests and SPIFFs appeal to the ego and achievement motivations of salespeople. When supported with frequent and ongoing feedback on individual or team results, contests and SPIFFs can also appeal to the social affiliation motivator by creating a sense of community among the participants. Contests and SPIFFs should be used in moderation so they don't confuse salespeople and divert attention away from strategic priorities. They also add to the complexity and cost of administering incentive programs. As a general rule, contests and SPIFFs should be used no more than two or three times per year and should constitute no more than 3% to 7% of total incentive spending.

Generational Diversity and Contests and SPIFFs

To create sales contests that appeal to a generationally diverse sales force, consider offering a choice of prizes. Although each individual is different, Baby Boomers are generally more likely to want tangible items (merchandise or a trophy), and Millennials are more likely to want experiences (trips or event tickets). One way to implement choice in contest prizes is to award gift card credits redeemable through an online catalog so winners can select the prizes they value most. Choice not only increases salespeople's motivation to participate in sales contests or SPIFFs but also eliminates the hassle of guessing which prizes people want and how many to preorder. Unlike cash prizes, catalog items and experiences can be personalized or customized so they are more meaningful and memorable than cash awards.

Millennials will engage more in contests and SPIFFs that are enabled by technology. Consider providing an app with an interactive dashboard, digital badges for reaching performance milestones or other fun motivational graphics.

Recognition Programs

Recognition programs showcase and reward the medium- and long-term performance of a company's best salespeople. These programs not only reward top performers but also model what success looks like for the rest of the sales force.

Most companies limit selection for recognition programs to the top 5% to 20% of performers on the basis of a combination of results metrics (quota achievement, sales growth) and behaviors consistent with long-term success (leadership, teamwork, customer focus). Salespeople who are recognized usually are invited to go on an exclusive trip, but the most important part of the recognition is the highlighting of their achievements before peers, management and customers. Often, this includes an invitation to join a select group, such as a President's Club, Inner Circle or Million Dollar Roundtable.

Recognition programs appeal especially to ego-driven salespeople. Because recognition programs often involve a trip or other group event, they can appeal to the social affiliation motivator as well.

Some forms of recognition are inexpensive. For example, Abbott Laboratories once put a star on the business cards of top sales performers.

Generational Diversity and Recognition Programs

Recognition of success has universal appeal across the generations, but there are some differences in the specifics of how each generation prefers to be recognized. More than younger generations, Baby Boomers often appreciate formal recognition in front of large groups and enjoy visible perks such as plaques and commemorative watches. Millennials may want recognition to be less formal but more frequent, and they often respond well to digital forms of recognition – for example, a manager or peer sharing kudos on the company intranet. Gen Xers also like recognition but are often most comfortable receiving the feedback privately or within a smaller group. In a survey ZS conducted of more than 500 salespeople in the United States, including an approximately equal number of salespeople from the Baby Boomer, Gen X and Millennial generations, salespeople's stated preferences for different forms of recognition showed that formal recognition programs, such as a President's Club, motivate most Baby Boomers but have much less impact on members of other generations.

Further Reading: "Generations in the Workforce & Marketplace: Preferences in Rewards, Recognition & Incentives" (Incentive Research Foundation).[8]

Sales Meetings and Events

Sales meetings, trips, in-person training and best practice sharing sessions, as well as other social events, appeal to the social affiliation motivator by fostering a connection to the company and to the sales team. Meetings are also an opportunity to communicate successes and, therefore, can appeal to the ego and achievement motivators.

An Environment That Motivates

Although incentive plans and supplemental motivation programs have a big influence on sales force motivation, these programs alone are not enough to motivate a sales force. Many aspects influence motivation.

Company Environment

Salespeople are more likely to be motivated when the company provides the following:

- clear direction and economically sound management
- a strong product or service portfolio

- good non-sales support for customers (customer service and delivery)
- strong marketing support (solid leads, high-impact sales materials)

Sales Force Environment

Nearly every sales force decision and program can influence motivation to some degree. Salespeople are more likely to be motivated when the sales force has the right:

- **Sales strategy:** People understand their role in achieving company goals and are enabled for success with the right value proposition, pricing and customer targeting.
- **Sales process and organization design:** People have roles that are within their bandwidth, sales territories that give them a fair opportunity to succeed and a sales process that enables success with customers.
- **Sales talent:** The company hires salespeople who are intrinsically motivated by the sales culture and develops them for success through excellent training and coaching.
- **Activity enablers:** Salespeople have the sales information they need, have realistic quotas and get appropriate feedback and encouragement from sales managers.
- **Sales force support:** The sales force gets strong administrative support (accurate sales tracking, efficient administrative processes, necessary data and tools).

Sales Culture

Culture is reflected in the norms, values and work style of the sales force. Certain sales force cultures will eventually dampen motivation. These include cultures that focus excessively on making short-term sales goals, cultures that allow salespeople to put personal financial gain ahead of customer and company success and cultures in which salespeople blame others and don't feel accountable for results.

Outside of these clearly "bad" cultures, many different sales force cultures can be effective, depending on the selling environment. Some cultures are competitive; others are cooperative. Some cultures empower salespeople to drive results; others focus on making sure salespeople engage in the right activities. Some cultures encourage risk taking; others encourage more risk-averse sales force behavior. What is important from a motivation perspective is that the sales culture aligns with the selling environment and with salespeople's beliefs, values and attitudes. Highly achievement-oriented and ego-driven salespeople are motivated by a results-focused culture, perhaps in which the sales force earns all its pay from commissions. Salespeople who have high social affiliation needs will find a team-oriented and collaborative culture motivating.

Conclusion

Diversity is a given in sales forces today, and this creates many challenges for designing incentive plans and motivating sales teams. The best sales force motivation programs embrace diversity by offering variety for people who have different motivational profiles.

The matrix in Figure 5-3 summarizes several of the sales force motivational programs discussed in this chapter and suggests which of these programs is most likely to appeal to each of the five universal motivators of salespeople. A periodic review of the programs you offer and their ability to affect different segments of your sales force helps to keep your motivation programs fresh and aligned with salespeople's needs.

Motivation Program	Motivational Need				
	Achievement	Social Affiliation	Power	Ego Gratification	Survival
Sales Incentive Plan	✔			✔	✔
Career Paths and Promotion Opportunities	✔		✔	✔	
Sales Contests and SPIFFs	✔	✔		✔	
Recognition Programs	✔	✔		✔	
Sales Meetings and Events	✔	✔		✔	

Figure 5-3. Programs Appealing to Salespeople With Different Motivational Needs

Endnotes

1   Andris A. Zoltners, Prabhakant Sinha and Greggor A. Zoltners, *The Complete Guide to Accelerating Sales Force Performance* (New York: AMACOM, 2001).

2   Chip Espinoza and Mick Ukleja, *Managing the Millennials: Discover the Core Competencies for Managing Today's Workforce,* 2nd ed. (Hoboken, NJ: John Wiley & Sons, 2016).

3   "Millennials Surpass Gen Xers as the Largest Generation in U.S. Labor Force," Richard Fry, Pew Research Center, May 11, 2015, http://www. pewresearch.org/fact-tank/2015/05/11/millennials-surpass-gen-xers-as-the-largest-generation-in-u-s-labor-force/ft_15-05-11_millennialsdefined/.

4   "Generations in the Workforce & Marketplace: Preferences in Rewards, Recognition & Incentives," Allan Schweyer, Incentive Research Foundation, July 21, 2015, http://theirf.org/research/generations-in-the-workforce-marketplacepreferences-in-rewards-recognition-incentives/1427/.

5   "How to Manage Different Generations," *Wall Street Journal,* http://guides.wsj. com/management/managing-your-people/how-to-manage-different-generations/.

6   Paul R. Lawrence and Nitin Nohria, *Driven: How Human Nature Shapes Our Choices* (San Francisco: Jossey-Bass, 2002).

7   Chad Albrecht and Steve Marley, *The Future of Sales Compensation* (Evanston, IL: ZS Associates, Inc., 2016).

8   "Generations in the Workforce & Marketplace."

CHAPTER 6

Driving Profit, Not Just Sales

Incentives That Drive Profitability

Companies expect salespeople to deliver not just sales but profitable sales growth. Often, salespeople have control over the profitability of sales either by influencing the price they offer customers or by allocating sales time across products with varying margins. Thus, it seems logical that when salespeople can influence profitability, incentive plans should link payouts to profitability metrics.

But it's not quite that simple. Too often, the complexity of calculations makes it difficult to track territory profitability in a timely and accurate fashion. Fortunately, as data and technology continue to advance, more companies are able to develop profitability metrics by salesperson.

A thoughtful approach to paying salespeople for profitability examines the desirability and feasibility of introducing profitability metrics (or surrogate measures of profitability) in sales incentive plans. In this chapter, we share insights into why, when and how to incentivize salespeople to generate more profitable sales.

The following examples describe companies from three different industries that changed their sales incentive compensation plans to improve profitability.

Industrial Lubricants

An industrial lubricants company historically paid its salespeople entirely through a commission on all sales in their territory. The plan fit well with the company's desire for simplicity and for keeping a constant cost of sales. As competition increased, salespeople began giving their customers deeper discounts and also stopped selling several higher-margin products that were difficult to sell in the more competitive environment. As profit margins dwindled, the company changed its incentive plan:

- **Before Change:** Pay 3% commission on sales.

- **After Change:** Pay 15% commission on gross margin.

The new message was clear and the impact immediate. Salespeople curtailed price discounts and focused more sales effort on profitable product lines. Although sales growth slowed down slightly, margin growth accelerated, and the change ultimately led to a significant increase in company profits.

Office Equipment

An office equipment maker gave its salespeople a dollar volume quota and paid them a 2% commission on sales up to quota and 5% above quota. Even though the company sold premium products, salespeople were quick to race to the bottom of the price range. Almost always, salespeople felt that selling a larger volume at a discount price would produce more sales dollars than selling a smaller volume at a premium price. Thus, they offered large discounts to build volume and get to the 5% commission level.

Salespeople were authorized to offer customers a 20% discount off list price, so they usually started pricing discussions at that level and then pushed their managers to approve additional discounts. The average actual selling price was 29% below list price. This not only hurt company profitability but also weakened the company's premium product image.

The company restructured its sales incentive plan as shown in Figure 6-1. The new plan linked commission rates to the percentage of list price that a customer paid.

One year later, the average discount dropped from 29% to 18%, and approximately 25% of orders were booked at list price, whereas virtually none had been before. Profits increased, and salespeople who were successful at holding price earned more commission. At the same time, compensation costs as a percentage of gross margin declined.

Before Change

Sales Level	Commission Rate on Sales
Up to quota	2.0%
Above quota	5.0%

After Change ———— Commission Rate on Sales ————

Sales Level	If More Than 20% Discount	If Up to 20% Discount	If No Discount
Up to quota	0.5%	1.5%	3.0%
Above quota	1.0%	3.0%	6.0%

Figure 6-1. Incentive Plan Change for an Office Equipment Maker

Medical Products

Salespeople at a medical device and supply company earned a commission on all sales. As a result of internal R&D efforts and acquisitions, the company continually added new products to the sales force's portfolio. Soon, salespeople lacked the time and bandwidth to sell everything. Many chose to focus within their comfort zone on the products that were most familiar or easy to sell. There was little incentive to learn how to sell several newer higher-margin products, even though executive leaders felt that these new products were strategically important to the company. To focus more sales force attention on these products, the company restructured the incentive plan by splitting products into separate groups on the basis of profitability, as shown in Figure 6-2. The strategic products grouping included newer products with an average 50% gross margin, and the core products grouping included older products with an average 30% gross margin.

As expected, the higher commission rate on strategic products led to an increase in sales of strategic products and higher profits for the company.

Why Pay Salespeople for Profitability?

It is no surprise that most sales incentive plans link pay to sales and revenue metrics. A salesperson's job is to create sales, and sales is the performance metric over which salespeople have the most influence. In

Before Change

Products	Commission Rate on Sales
All	3.5%

After Change

Products	Commission Rate on Sales
Core	2.5%
Strategic	5.0%

Figure 6-2. Incentive Plan Change for a Medical Device and Supply Company

addition, for most companies, measuring sales for each salesperson is straightforward, and the metric is easy for the sales force to understand.

Some companies will argue that salespeople should be paid on profitability because that's how senior leaders are measured and that's what investors require. However, paying on profitability can add unnecessary complexity to an incentive plan and in many sales force circumstances produces little or no benefit.

If your company's priorities focus on driving *profitable* sales and your *salespeople have control over the gross margin of sales*, then you can improve financial performance by linking sales incentive compensation to profitability. Consider the following examples that demonstrate the financial impact that salespeople's actions can have on profitability.

First, when salespeople can influence the price they offer customers, the right incentives can encourage salespeople to sell at a higher price and avoid discounting. The example in Figure 6-3 demonstrates the

	List Price	5% Discount	5% Premium	
Price	$100	$95	$105	→ 5% swing
Cost of Goods Sold	–$70	–$70	–$70	
Margin	$30	$25	$35	→ 17% swing
Selling, General & Administrative Expense	–$20	–$20	–$20	
Net Profit	$10	$5	$15	→ 50% swing

Figure 6-3. The Value of Selling at a Higher Price

magnified impact that price has on margin and net profit. Selling at a higher price often requires more sales effort. However, in this example, *if a salesperson can sell at a higher or a lower price with roughly equal sales effort*, then a 5% price swing leads to a 17% margin swing and a 50% net profit swing.

Second, when salespeople are empowered to allocate sales time as they choose across products that have different margins, the right incentives can drive sales activity toward more profitable products. The example shown in Figure 6-4 demonstrates the impact that selling a higher-margin product has on net profit. Selling a higher-margin product often requires more sales effort than selling a lower-margin product. However, in this example, *if a salesperson can sell either the strategic or the core products with roughly equal sales effort*, then selling the strategic products rather than the core products produces 150% higher net profit for the company. If selling the higher margin requires more sales effort, then the profit impact is less.

When to Pay for Profitability

Paying salespeople for profitability doesn't make sense for every sales force. It is effective in situations in which profitability is strategic and is within the sales force's control. Assess your situation by answering two key questions. If the answer to both of these questions is "yes," then your company should consider linking sales compensation to a profitability metric.

	Core Products (30% Margin)	Strategic Products (37.5% Margin, 20% Price Premium)	
Price	$100	$120	→ 20% higher
Cost of Goods Sold	-$70	-$75	
Margin	$30	$45	→ 50% higher
Selling, General & Administrative Expense	-$20	-$20	
Net Profit	$10	$25	→ 150% higher

Figure 6-4. The Value of Selling Higher-Margin Products

Question 1: Is Paying Salespeople for Profitability Strategic?

Profitability is often a strategic goal for companies, but not always. Companies may sacrifice profitability for a number of reasons – to build market share, to block a competitor or to gain entry into a new market. Consider paying salespeople for profitability only if profitability is aligned with your company's strategy. If profitability is not your objective, then choose an incentive plan metric that aligns with what you hope to achieve, such as market share, competitive wins or revenue growth.

Question 2: Can Salespeople Control Profitability?

Salespeople can control profitability to some extent by minimizing costs, such as by controlling their expenses for travel and administration. Linking sales force incentives to profitability is most effective, however, when salespeople can influence the gross margin of sales. Not all salespeople have this ability. For example, salespeople who sell a single product at a set price have no impact on gross margin; the way they increase profits is by increasing sales. Thus, there is nothing to be gained by paying on gross margin; the result will be the same as paying on sales.

Salespeople have the ability to affect gross margin in two primary situations – when they can influence price and when they sell multiple products with varied margins. Assess your situation by answering the following questions.

Can Salespeople Influence the Price They Offer Customers?

Salespeople directly affect the gross margin of sales when they can set price. Companies have different philosophies about whether salespeople should have pricing authority. Some give salespeople a lot of leeway to negotiate price, arguing that salespeople have the best knowledge of a customer's needs and willingness to pay. Others give the sales force no say in pricing decisions, arguing that pricing is a strategic decision and that salespeople will too often cut price to make sales. Some companies distribute pricing authority. For example, they might give salespeople the ability to discount up to 5% while giving sales managers authority to discount up to 10%, with larger discounts requiring the approval of headquarters. The more pricing authority the sales force has, the larger its ability to influence profitability, and the greater the benefit of linking incentives to profits rather than revenues.

Can Salespeople Sell Multiple Products With Varying Margins?

Salespeople who sell multiple products can almost always influence the amount of time they spend promoting each product. If all products in the portfolio have a similar profit margin (and salespeople can't affect price), then there is little benefit to paying incentives on gross margin; the result will be the same as paying on sales.

However, when products have widely varied gross margins, incentives linked to profitability metrics can direct sales force effort to more profitable product lines. The more opportunity a sales force has to allocate sales time across products with varying margins, the larger its ability to influence the gross margin of sales, and the greater the benefit of linking incentives to profitability.

How to Incentivize Profitable Sales

The company examples at the start of this chapter illustrate three different approaches for linking sales incentive compensation to profitability:

1. **Pay on gross margin dollars** like the industrial lubricants company.

2. **Pay on average selling price** like the office equipment maker.

3. **Pay on product grouping** like the medical device and supply company.

The best approach depends on whether territory gross margin is measurable and whether the company is willing to share margin information with the sales force. It also depends on how salespeople influence gross margin. Figure 6-5 provides a decision tree to help you evaluate your situation.

Pay on Gross Margin if You Can Measure It at the Territory Level

If your company can and wants to measure gross margin at the territory level, then paying on territory gross margin is the most straightforward way to encourage salespeople to sell at a high price or to emphasize higher-margin products. The approach is simple in concept and is easy for salespeople to understand.

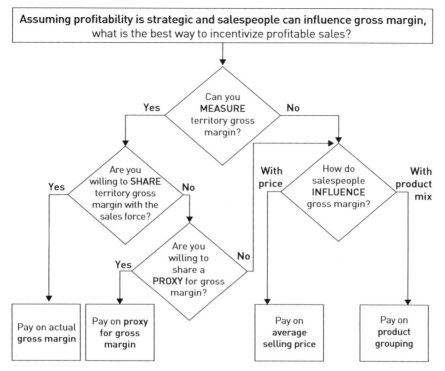

Figure 6-5. Decision Tree for Determining How to Drive Price or Margin With Incentives

Pay on Actual Gross Margin if the Information Is Sharable With the Sales Force

If protecting the confidentiality of margins is not important and you are comfortable sharing gross margin information with salespeople, then use gross margin as the metric for determining incentive pay, instead of using sales or revenues. The adjustment required to the incentive plan depends on what type of plan you have. For example:

- **With a commission plan:** Adjust the commission rate appropriately. You will need to pay a higher rate on gross margin than you paid on sales. The example in the inset box provides insight about how to make the appropriate adjustment to the commission rate.

- **With a quota-based plan:** You will need to adjust your quota setting process. Set a territory gross margin quota (instead of a sales quota) for each salesperson. Link incentive pay to gross margin quota achievement instead of linking it to sales quota achievement.

Example: Adjusting a Commission Rate on Sales to a Rate on Gross Margin

Determining the right commission rate when moving from a sales-based to a margin-based incentive plan is not as simple as it appears. There is a rate on gross margin that is mathematically equivalent to the rate on revenue. Consider the example shown in Figure 6-6 for a salesperson who produces $5 million in sales at an average 20% gross margin.

You may also want to account for the fact that the incentive plan change will have an impact on sales force behavior and margin results. In our example, if salespeople get paid 15% on margin rather than 3% on sales, they should begin to focus on more profitable sales. The average gross margin may increase to more than 20%. The company will benefit from improved margin performance, but it will also have to pay out more in incentives.

Consider whether this increase in incentive costs (effectively a raise for the sales force) is a desired outcome. If it's not, set the commission rate on gross margin to a rate that results in the appropriate sales force pay level. In our example, you might set the rate on gross margin at 14% rather than 15% to limit the increase in sales compensation costs.

Consider Paying on Margin Proxy if You Want to Protect the Confidentiality of Margins

Some companies, especially in high-margin businesses, want to protect the confidentiality of their profit margins. Therefore, they don't want to share margins with salespeople, who might share the information with customers or might switch companies and share margins with

Commission on Sales	=	Commission on Gross Margin
$5 million sales		$5 million sales × 20% margin = $1 million gross margin
× 3% commission rate		× 15% commission rate
= $150,000 commission		= $150,000 commission

Figure 6-6. Example Calculation of Mathematically Equivalent Commission Rates on Sales and Gross Margin

competitors. You can address margin confidentiality issues by using margin proxies for incentive compensation. These artificially calculated margins reflect the relative profitability of products without revealing actual margins. Margin proxies do, however, reveal information to salespeople. Thus, if you are very concerned about protecting margin confidentiality, consider instead paying on product grouping or average selling price, as described later in the chapter.

Address the Challenges of Measuring Territory Gross Margin

Unfortunately, measuring and reporting gross margin at the territory level is often more difficult than it seems. At least two situations can make the cost of measuring and reporting territory gross margin too great.

First, in some businesses, margins are sometimes so high that there is little value to measuring and paying on margin. Paying on margin is almost the same as paying on revenues. The extra effort and complexity involved in tracking and paying on margins simply isn't worth it.

Second, some companies find it challenging to measure margins down to the territory level. Even if systems allow measurement, complex calculations can make it difficult to gain sales force understanding and acceptance of gross margin metrics.

When a medical device company started paying commissions on margins instead of sales, constant change in product costs, distribution costs, product rebates and portfolio rebates made it a nightmare to determine territory-level margins. The plan was abandoned after just one quarter. To avoid this problem, some companies will develop a set of constant product costs to use for calculating territory margins, thus eliminating the variability.

Fortunately, advances in data and technology are enabling many companies to develop more streamlined systems for measuring margins at the territory level. One information technology services company recently implemented a new information system that allowed it to measure margins at the account level for the first time. Before the system upgrade, salespeople had no idea of what the margins of their sales were. The new visibility into the profitability of every service at every account prompted salespeople to begin engaging in more profitable selling activities. When the company reinforced this by changing the incentive plan to link incentive payouts to a margin-based rather than a sales-based metric, overall margin improved significantly.

Pay on Average Selling Price or Product Grouping if You Can't Measure Territory Gross Margin

If you can't or don't want to measure or share gross margin at the territory level, then paying on average selling price or product grouping can encourage more profitable selling.

Pay on Average Selling Price to Discourage Discounting

For sales forces that have pricing authority, paying on territory gross margin encourages salespeople to sell at a high price. However, if the cost of measuring and sharing territory gross margin is too great, an average selling price approach is a good alternative for linking incentives to profitability.

Incentive plans that link payout to average selling price encourage salespeople to sell as much as possible at the highest possible price. The incentive plan shown in Figure 6-7 is a commission plan with a multiplier linked to average selling price performance. This plan is appropriate when you want to pay a commission but want to discourage salespeople from conceding price in order to outperform on volume.

Pay on Product Grouping to Drive Sales of Higher-Margin Products

For sales forces that sell multiple products with different margins, paying on territory gross margin encourages salespeople to focus on high-margin products. However, if the cost of measuring and sharing territory gross margin is too great, then paying on product grouping is a good alternative for linking incentives to profitability.

Paying on product grouping encourages salespeople to spend time on more profitable or strategically important products. The incentive plan shown in Figure 6-8 uses this approach with commissions that

Average Selling Price Performance	Definition	Commission Rate Multiplier
Excellent	Sell 3% or more above list price	1.25×
Target	Sell at list price plus or minus 3%	1.10×
Below Target	Sell 3% or more below list price	1.00×

Figure 6-7. A Commission Plan for Driving Average Selling Price Performance

Products	Commission Rate on Sales up to Quota	Commission Rate on Sales Above Quota
Premium	5.0%	11.0%
Core	2.5%	5.0%

Figure 6-8. A Commission Plan for Driving Quota Achievement and Focus on Premium Products

accelerate once sales reach a territory quota. Commission rates vary to reflect differences in the margins and strategic importance of premium versus core products.

Creative Approaches: More Examples of Incentive Plans That Reinforce Profitability Objectives

There are many creative ways to use the approaches described in this chapter to design an incentive plan that aligns with company profitability objectives. Here are two additional examples from the many possible plans for incentivizing profitable sales.

Example 1: Commission on Gross Margin With Accelerator for Premium Product Achievement

The plan shown in Figure 6-9 pays a base commission rate on the gross margin dollars of all products sold. Salespeople get an overall quota and a separate quota for a grouping of premium, higher-margin products. The commission rate accelerates when salespeople hit their overall gross

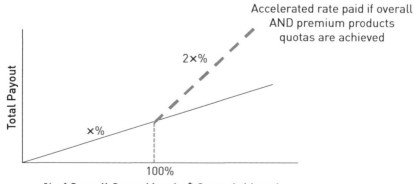

Figure 6-9. A Commission Plan for Driving Margin and Encouraging Focus on Premium Products

margin quota and also hit their premium products quota. This gives salespeople incentive to make their overall quota but to do it in a way that's aligned with company priorities – by focusing on premium products. The only way to get the accelerated rate is to hit both the overall quota and the premium products quota. Linking the accelerator to an overall quota and a premium quota (rather than linking it to a core quota and a premium quota, such as in the example in Figure 6-8) eliminates any penalty for not hitting the quota on non-premium or core products and keeps the focus on the premium products.

This plan is appropriate when you want salespeople to sell higher-price or higher-margin products that are replacements for existing lower-price or lower-margin products.

Example 2: Commission Rate Varies With the Gross Margin of Each Transaction

The plan shown in Figure 6-10 is used by a distributor to drive gross margin while reinforcing the relative strategic importance of its products. Salespeople earn a core commission rate equal to the gross margin percentage achieved on each transaction. This gives salespeople significant incentive to sell high-margin deals. To encourage focus on strategically important products, the commission rate accelerates to the gross margin percentage plus 5% for premium product sales. The inset box shows an example incentive pay calculation for this plan.

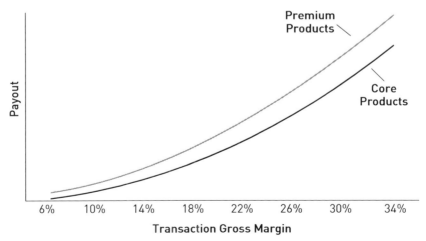

Figure 6-10. An Alternative Commission Plan for Driving Margin and Encouraging Focus on Premium Products

Example: Incentive Pay Calculation for the Figure 6-10 Plan

Say a salesperson sells $20,000 in core product revenue at 25% gross margin. He or she earns a 25% core commission (equal to the gross margin percentage) on the gross margin dollars generated by the deal. The salesperson's commission is calculated as follows:

- $20,000 sale × 25% gross margin = $5,000 gross margin

- $5,000 gross margin × 25% core commission rate = $1,250 incentive

If the salesperson sells the same $20,000 core products deal at 30% gross margin, he or she earns:

- $20,000 sale × 30% gross margin = $6,000 gross margin

- $6,000 gross margin × 30% core commission rate = $1,800 incentive

There is a multiplicative effect – the gross margin dollars in the second example are 1.2 times the gross margin dollars in the first example, but the commission earned is 1.44 times more.

This plan is appropriate when it's very important that salespeople drive the highest margin on every transaction and there are many transactions. Plans such as this one have been used successfully in the distribution industry and elsewhere.

Conclusion

Sales incentive compensation plans play a key role in reinforcing company strategy. Consequently, when strategies change, sales compensation plans also need to change to stay aligned. Many companies today are implementing sales strategies focused on margin improvement, while giving salespeople the opportunity to affect margin either by influencing the price they offer customers or by allocating sales time across products with varying margins. As enhancements in data and systems make it easier to measure profitability at the territory level consistently, there are new opportunities for these companies to adapt their sales incentive plans to drive more profitable sales.

CHAPTER 7

Going Global With Sales Compensation

What Is a Globalized Sales Incentive Compensation Program?

There is a debate among leaders of global sales organizations about the value of creating consistency in sales incentive compensation plans across countries. A senior compensation leader at a global hardware technology firm argued that it's best to have a single global plan for each sales role:

> "A global sales incentive plan aligns with the needs of global customers and creates uniformly effective and fair compensation for everyone. A global plan provides a greater degree of control over sales incentive spending around the world, simplifies plan management, and enables efficiencies in plan administration."

A senior sales leader at the same firm believed that a single global sales incentive plan per sales role could not work. He argued:

> "Sales is essentially a local function. It works differently across countries, due to variations in market maturity, channel structures, product portfolios, and other market dynamics, as well as differences in the business culture and laws, and the availability of data for measuring performance. Global diversity makes a one-size-fits-all sales incentive compensation plan impractical and ineffective."

Increasingly, global companies are discovering that both of these arguments have merit. So the issue becomes how you can realize the benefits of a globalized sales compensation program without losing the flexibility required to meet local needs.

A globalized sales compensation program can be implemented in different ways. Some global companies are implementing either or both of the following approaches:

1. **Consistent incentive plan design** in terms of the pay mix, metrics, plan type, payout curve and other plan design features for salespeople in different countries who perform similar sales roles

2. **Centralized resources** for helping countries design and implement changes to local incentive plans or for administering incentive plans

This chapter will describe each of these approaches to globalized sales incentive programs, along with their advantages and challenges. By sharing examples and advice, this chapter can help you figure out whether either or both of these approaches make sense for your situation, and if so, how to go about implementing a globalized program.

Globalizing Incentive Plan Design

Plan design globalization creates consistency in incentive plan features for salespeople in different countries who perform similar sales roles. In its strictest form, global plan design means that there is a single global plan for each sales role with no exceptions. This is quite rare, however, because it is almost always necessary to create a plan that accounts for some differences across countries.

One company had account managers who played the same sales role in every country. Account managers earned a salary plus an incentive component that was determined by a plan that aligned with the global definition for the account manager role.

Regardless of location, the incentive portion of an account manager's pay was a bonus linked to individual attainment of a revenue quota weighted at 70% plus a commission on new sales weighted at 30%. The company used a global oversight approach for allowing exceptions to the plan on the basis of local circumstances (see more about this later in the chapter).

Benefits of Globalizing Incentive Plan Design

There are three main benefits to a global sales incentive plan design:

1. **Alignment with global selling models:** To meet the needs of customers with global buying processes, selling companies may need global sales processes. For example, a global customer of a large technology company wants to purchase and implement the same hardware and software solution in multiple locations around the world. This requires the technology company to execute a global sales process with people in the same sales roles deployed to each country to implement the solution locally. It is logical that everyone in the same role should get paid in a consistent manner.

2. **Fairness and appropriateness:** A global plan design can keep sales force pay in all countries aligned with the value of the sales role and treat people fairly across countries, ensuring that no one gets paid inappropriately because of a local management bias.

3. **Simplified plan management and administration:** A global plan simplifies plan management and makes it easier to centralize plan administration (more on the benefits of centralizing administration later in this chapter). It can also enable more rapid plan design and deployment – for example, in support of a new product or service launch.

Challenges of Globalizing Plan Design

The challenges for globalizing incentive plan design are that market dynamics (and therefore sales roles), cultures, laws and data availability can vary across countries.

Different Market Dynamics

Differences in market dynamics can result from several factors. These include:

- **Market maturity:** A technology company had salespeople in many countries. The global sales role definition called for all salespeople to both support existing customers and develop new accounts. Market maturity differences across countries led to variations in how much time salespeople spent on each of these activities. The company's products had matured in the U.S. market (single-digit growth) but were experiencing 40% growth rates in China. Thus, salespeople in the United States spent more time protecting business with existing customers, whereas in China salespeople spent more time on new customer acquisition.

- **Channel structures:** A technology company goes to market in the United States using face-to-face selling supplemented by inside sales. In Asia, it sells through distributors.

- **Product portfolios:** Differences in the products sold across markets can lead to different target audiences, value propositions and sales processes across countries.

These market differences can create a need for different sales roles. Addressing these and other sources of market diversity is a significant challenge for designing a global sales incentive plan.

Different Cultures

Culture concerning incentive pay differs across countries. Figure 7-1 illustrates some incentive plan design differences across countries at a global manufacturing company. These differences resulted from business culture dissimilarities and not from a difference in sales strategy or products across countries. In the United States, where the business culture emphasizes individual performance, 35% of salespeople's pay comes from incentives tied to individually based metrics. In Japan, where the business culture stresses teamwork, just 15% of salespeople's pay comes from incentives, with the amount determined in part by team performance. In Nordic countries, where the business culture favors protection from risk (relative to business cultures such as the United States that favor higher risk for higher reward), only 10% of pay comes from

Country	Salary:Incentive Mix	Individual or Team	Payout Frequency
United States	65:35	Individual	Monthly
Nordic Countries	90:10	Individual	Annual
Japan	85:15	Team and Individual	Semiannual

Figure 7-1. Incentive Plan Design by Country at a Global Manufacturing Company

incentives linked to individual performance. Differences in pay mix also lead to differences in payout frequency across countries.

Multiplying this diversity by the many dozens of countries that this company sold to, it's understandable why it can be challenging to create a single incentive plan that works in every country.

Different Laws

Differences across countries in governmental regulations and restrictions, as well as in the influence of labor unions and work councils, can affect incentive practices. In some countries, laws affecting sales compensation may restrict the ability of a sales force to make base pay reductions. In countries such as Germany, work councils may have to approve sales compensation plan changes. Countries also have different regulations about issues such as employment contracts, incentive pay caps, overtime pay, mandatory increases and the ability to change incentive plans or quotas without employee consent. Addressing these and other sources of legal diversity is a significant challenge for designing a global sales incentive plan.

Different Data Availability

Data availability can differ across markets. When one technology company sought to globalize its incentive compensation plan, it discovered that data capturing end-user sales from distributors were not available in all markets, making it impossible to measure the performance of the salespeople in some countries using individual revenue as a metric.

Making Global Plan Design Work

Not every global sales force should have a global sales incentive plan. Global plan design is a good idea only when market dynamics enable similar sales processes and roles around the world and when a single plan has enough flexibility to acknowledge differences in culture, laws and data availability across countries.

A technology company provided countries with flexibility by incorporating a local component in the global plan design. The company sold products and services in more than 75 countries to large corporate customers who often wanted to install the same software in all their worldwide locations. Thus, the company used the same roles and sales processes in every country.

Prior to the globalization initiative, the company had hundreds of separate sales incentive plans. To design a single global plan, the company established a global incentive plan design team, gathered input from local country teams and created a plan design and pay mix for each sales role that could work in every country. To acknowledge local differences, the global plan included a local component. Each country had flexibility to set objectives for salespeople that reflected the country's unique selling situation and could pay up to 15% of the incentive portion of pay on the basis of the achievement of those objectives.

In addition to aligning with the company's global selling model and providing fair and appropriate sales incentive pay in all countries, the global plan enabled centralization of incentive plan administration. This reduced costs by allowing the company to eliminate more than half of the incentive compensation administration staff located in two regional processing centers. The initiative created big efficiency improvements, without sacrificing the effectiveness of incentives to motivate sales force behavior across the globe.

Companies can provide different degrees of flexibility for countries to deviate from a global plan design. Examples here illustrate approaches at both ends of the flexibility spectrum:

- **A global oversight approach** gives countries very limited flexibility to adapt a global plan on the basis of local needs.

- **A global guidelines approach** provides suggestions rather than strict rules for countries to follow.

In most situations, a global guidelines approach works best because it allows countries to meet diverse local needs while at the same time helping them align plans to a global compensation strategy and philosophy.

A Global Oversight Approach

Recall the company described earlier in this chapter that had a global sales incentive plan for its account managers. The plan had a bonus linked to attainment of a revenue quota weighted at 70% and a commission on new sales weighted at 30%. If a country felt that its unique circumstances made the global plan inappropriate, it could request an exception subject to the approval of a global sales compensation committee. For example, Japan asked that the plan link to team, rather than individual, performance, in order to align with the team-based sales approach used in Japan.

A Global Guidelines Approach

When a medical device company sought greater global consistency in the pay plan for its new business development salespeople, it created a set of guiding principles for countries to follow when designing their incentive plans. Within the context of the global guidelines, countries had flexibility to control many details of the incentive plan design. That way, countries could make incentive plan design choices that reflected local needs but also aligned with global company sales and compensation strategies and philosophies. The global guidelines are shown in Figure 7-2.

After rolling out these global guidelines, the company saw significant improvement in the quality and consistency of incentive plan design across countries. This simplified the administrative process and provided better visibility into global plan performance.

In most situations, the dynamics of selling vary across the world. A global guidelines approach allows countries to design incentive plans that fit with their local needs, laws and culture while also aligning with a unified company perspective. In most cases, this is the best approach to global sales compensation plan design.

Key Incentive Plan Design Decisions	Global Guideline
Target Pay Level	Match 60th percentile of local market on the basis of benchmarking.
Salary:Incentive Mix	Match local market salary:incentive mix on the basis of benchmarking.
Performance Metrics	Pay on revenues (specific timing determined locally). Pay for individual (not team) performance. Pay for management by objectives (MBO) achievement rarely at a salesperson level; maximum allowable is 20% of incentive.
Performance-Payout Relationship	Pay commission, no thresholds, no caps or decelerators.
Performance Period and Payment Frequency	Tie plan to annual performance, with payment frequency tied to local salary:incentive mix.

Figure 7-2. Incentive Plan Guiding Principles for an Example Medical Device New Business Development Sales Force

Supporting Global Incentive Programs With Centralized Resources

As large global companies seek to bring expertise and efficiency to the design and administration of sales incentive plans across countries, more are creating centralized resources for supporting their global sales incentive compensation programs. These resources can include people, processes, data and tools. Centralized resources can benefit companies that have a global plan design, as well as those that allow each country to design its incentive plan independently (although the second case is less common). Through exposure to many situations and nuances, a centralized global team can develop a deep understanding of the issues involved in designing and administering a global sales incentive program. Because of the experience and knowledge gained through repetition and practice, and the observation of what works in many diverse situations, a global team can often do a better job of executing these tasks than can a collection of isolated individuals or teams working in different countries.

Centralized resources can fill two different global incentive compensation program needs: plan design and plan administration.

A Global Center of Excellence for Incentive Plan Design

Some large global companies have improved the design of sales incentive plans around the world by establishing a global center of excellence or expertise (COE). The COE acts as a resource to help countries design and implement effective change in their sales incentive plans.

Global Plan Design Resources at GE

When GE first implemented a cross-organizational initiative aimed at enhancing global sales force effectiveness, variable incentive compensation was a key area of focus. A sales force effectiveness director at global headquarters was charged with bringing excellence to incentive compensation (and other sales force decisions) in GE businesses around the world. The initiative included the following:

- developing a consistent set of frameworks, models, capabilities and best practices for all GE businesses to use

- propagating best practices across GE businesses through training and education

- serving as a resource by providing wisdom, experience and project team members who could help businesses execute the frameworks

- improving the frameworks, models and approaches continually in order to ensure ongoing progress in global commercial excellence

These global resources helped many GE businesses assess the effectiveness of their sales incentive compensation plans, improve alignment with pay for performance, evaluate the strength of payout controls and build communication plans for implementing successful plan change. A project for one business – GE Capital Solutions – resulted in a reduction in the number of plans from 165 to 69. The project also achieved 90% compliance with global incentive plan guidelines that increased focus on pay for performance and profitability.

Benefits of a Global Center of Incentive Plan Design Excellence

A global COE can help to ensure that sales incentive plans across all countries reflect sufficient knowledge about incentive compensation theory and practice, while aligning with a unified corporate incentive compensation philosophy. Differences in plan design across countries are a good idea to the extent that plans reflect differences in local needs and culture.

Too often, however, locally designed plans differ simply because of the varied expertise of local management teams or differences in personal philosophies that aren't aligned with an overarching company culture and strategy. Ultimately, an effective COE helps all countries design and implement better incentive plans that will motivate higher levels of sales force performance.

Challenges to Creating a Global COE That Gets Results

A global COE represents a significant investment, so companies need sufficient global scale to justify an investment in resources. Typically, to make a large-scale COE cost-effective, a company needs to sell in multiple countries that deploy a minimum of several hundred salespeople across multiple sales roles. Smaller global sales forces can benefit from a smaller-scale investment – perhaps a small group of advisors on the global staff.

In addition, countries need to see value in using the COE. This means that the COE needs resources and expertise that are compelling and appropriate to each country's needs. Resources can include:

- insightful leadership and project teams of capable individuals
- best practice knowledge, including information gathered from both inside and outside the company
- decision frameworks and processes that local teams can relate to and that lead to better incentive plan design and implementation choices

The best role for a COE is not to dictate answers but to work with countries to find answers that acknowledge local dynamics and also reflect understanding from a company and compensation theory and practice perspective. A COE is most effective when local management teams view it as a resource and not as an attempt by headquarters to exert control. Of course, some control is necessary for companies that want global consistency in plan design. However, even in cases in which the COE helps to provide oversight and ensure alignment with global guidelines, the COE will be most effective if its personnel have the respect of sales leaders across countries and treat local country personnel as customers, not as resources that they control.

When one company established a global incentive plan design COE, the initiative was not unanimously embraced across the world. Although some countries welcomed the advice and resources provided by the global team, others resisted headquarters coming in and dictating how to run their business. A sales leader in China said, "Our market is growing fast; many of the people in the COE come from mature markets and they can't relate to our challenges." In some European countries, local managers felt "the analysts in the COE don't understand our culture." In the end, many countries did make use of the global team resources, but the overall benefits realized were much less than expected.

Centralized Resources for Administering Incentive Plans

There can be a considerable downside in going too far with standardizing sales incentive plan *design* across countries. However, when it comes to plan *administration*, the advantages of standardization are significant. With incentive plan administration costs typically adding 2% to 15% to total incentive compensation costs, streamlining and centralizing administration can create considerable cost savings.

Benefits of Centralizing Incentive Plan Administration

Incentive plan administration is often complex and error prone, and many companies don't do a very good job of it. The challenge is especially large in complex situations (for example, many sales roles, performance metrics, data sources, rules about exceptions) and when a desire for flexibility (for example, midstream adjustments in sales crediting, territory alignment and plan eligibility) introduces opportunities for errors.

Companies with complex plans and flexible processes make many errors in plan administration. Small errors occur frequently. Big errors can occur, too, leading to sales force distrust and undermining the power of the incentive plan to motivate.

Provided there is sufficient scale, most companies can benefit from centralizing and streamlining as much of their incentive plan administration as possible. The benefits include:

- **Cost savings:** Centralized incentive compensation plan administration is more efficient. Redundant resources across countries are eliminated, leading to substantial cost savings. In addition, it is often possible to find highly skilled people in lower-cost labor markets who can do the work.

- **Increased administrative effectiveness:** Consistency in data collection and reporting and the creation and use of operational best practices reduce the number of errors and contribute to administrative effectiveness gains.

- **Risk mitigation:** Centralizing the administration of compensation plans can help mitigate risk. Headquarters can more easily track incentive plan spending; get visibility into anticipated incentive costs and results by country; and identify problems early, before payouts go out to local sales teams and it's too late to make adjustments. Global oversight also makes it easier to comply with regulatory requirements, such as Sarbanes-Oxley in the United States.

Examples of the Impact

One large financial company had more than 700 salespeople in more than 50 countries across the globe. When the company centralized its sales incentive plan administration, it estimated that the change created an 11% cost reduction by streamlining processes and eliminating activities that were redundant across regions. In addition, distrust of the old support systems had caused salespeople and managers to spend as much as 10% of their time checking the accuracy of the data and calculations used for determining incentive payouts. The new and improved system increased sales force trust in the administrative process and eliminated almost all of the shadow accounting, leading to an increase in sales manager coaching and salesperson selling time.

At another global company, each country historically had its own local team responsible for administering the sales compensation program. Plans across countries were similar, although not identical, with almost all countries using one of three basic plan designs. Countries administered their plans by using locally designed spreadsheet file formats and processes.

Larger countries, such as the United States, had dedicated people who performed this work. Smaller countries across Europe, Latin America and Asia had part-time people who performed these duties one week a month and then returned to other job responsibilities, often in finance or human resources. For a while, the decentralized process worked, and country sales leaders liked having a local administration team available to produce customized reports on request. However, as the company grew and the complexity of the sales compensation program increased, the fragmented and fractionalized approach, particularly outside of the United States, became inefficient, and the quality was inconsistent across countries.

The company decided to centralize sales compensation administration. Working with an outside partner, it selected a flexible web-based software solution that all countries could use to manage the incentive administration process and ensure payouts were correct and on time. The partner initially provided managed services support but eventually transitioned this responsibility to the company's own service center in India. There, a centralized team administered incentive plans for more than 45 countries. The result was a more reliable and efficient process for collecting and reporting data, with consistent creation and execution of operational best practices.

Challenges to Making Centralized Plan Administration Work

The resources required for centralizing plan administration can be significant. The return on the investment will be faster for companies that have large global scale – typically multiple countries that deploy a minimum of several hundred salespeople across multiple sales roles. A good return on investment also requires that many countries are willing to use the centralized services. Having a central budget for helping local markets pay the initial setup costs can help encourage adoption.

Strong adoption by local countries also requires effective communication between sales forces across the globe and the centralized incentive plan administration staff. There are language and cultural barriers to overcome. Local countries may feel that responsiveness and the ability to implement changes quickly are reduced. A strategy that can work for improving sensitivity to local needs and minimizing the perception of an overly centralized process is to place a local, on-the-ground resource in major countries or regions – an individual who has the ability to see the world through the lens of both the local sales force and the centralized administrative staff. This individual speaks both languages (both literally and figuratively) and can earn the trust and respect of people in both groups, while effectively managing communication flows between the groups.

Managing time differences can be challenging. With local plan administration, sales force members may become accustomed to getting a quick response to their queries, but when administration is centralized and performed on the other side of the globe, the response time gets longer. Sales force members may need to adjust their expectations for responsiveness and adapt the way they work accordingly. Time zone differences can also complicate the scheduling of system maintenance. Creative approaches to scheduling system downtime ensure that sales force members get access to critical data during local business hours. Another way to address time zone differences is to set up multiple administrative centers in different parts of the world.

Conclusion

Companies with large global sales forces can benefit from initiatives aimed at enhancing the effectiveness of salespeople around the world. Such initiatives can include a globalized sales incentive compensation program, which companies can approach in different ways. Two common approaches are:

1. **Global plan design:** a single incentive plan for each sales role globally
2. **Centralized resources:** global expertise and resources to help countries design or administer incentive programs

Depending on your circumstances and needs, either or both of these approaches can produce benefits. When globalizing plan design, companies should tread with care. The varied dynamics of selling around the world make it necessary to create some flexibility in the global plan design to allow it to work well in every country. An approach that often works is to create global guiding principles that encourage countries to make plan design choices that align with a unified company perspective but also fit with local needs and culture.

When centralizing resources for designing or administering incentive plans, companies can realize many benefits, provided there is sufficient scale, as well as empathy, for local issues. Global resources can offer incentive plan design expertise to help countries create plans that meet local needs and also reflect best practice incentive compensation knowledge. In addition, by centralizing plan administration, companies can reduce administrative costs and create effectiveness gains while also enabling better global oversight of sales compensation spending.

A globalized approach to sales incentive compensation is not right for every sales force, but when implemented in the right circumstances and in the right way, globalization can increase both the effectiveness and the efficiency of a global sales incentive compensation program.

CHAPTER 8

Using Analytics to Boost Sales Compensation Impact

Understanding the Opportunity of Analytics

In the last decade, the availability and quality of data have increased immensely, and information systems are providing a platform for greater and more flexible analytic capabilities. More and more companies are seeking to take advantage of this innovation to boost the ongoing impact of their sales compensation plans. When implemented effectively, the ongoing use of analytics can give sales managers and salespeople powerful feedback about their performance, thus increasing sales force engagement in an incentive plan. In addition, analytics can help sales and compensation leaders continually diagnose sales compensation plan effectiveness and identify potential problems in time to make course corrections.

More and more companies are becoming aware of the power of using analytics to improve sales compensation plan performance. However, with all the data, systems and analytical tools available today, it can be difficult to know where to start. As a result, the use of analytics to boost sales compensation plan impact is an underrealized opportunity for many sales forces.

This chapter shares ideas for using analytics and information technology to enhance the power of a sales compensation plan in two main ways:

1. **Providing salespeople and managers with ongoing feedback** about performance in order to motivate and engage the sales force

2. **Performing plan health checks to help sales and compensation leaders** regularly diagnose sales compensation plan performance and bring about continual sales force improvement

Ongoing Feedback to Motivate Salespeople and Managers

Enabled by today's rapidly evolving information systems and analytic capabilities, companies can provide salespeople and managers with more timely and powerful feedback about their performance and its impact on sales compensation, thereby increasing the motivational power of a sales compensation plan.

Feedback Motivates

Marketing professors Joseph C. Nunes and Xavier Drèze[1] conducted a field research experiment aimed at testing certain dynamics affecting the effort people will exert toward reaching goals. The experiment took place at a professional car wash. Customers were given cards entitling them to a free wash after a certain number of visits. When the researchers tracked return visits for these customers, they discovered that as customers got closer to their free wash, they began to get their cars washed more frequently. The time between visits decreased on average by about half a day with each additional car wash purchased. Progress toward the goal motivated customers to try harder to reach the goal.

Just like the car wash customers, salespeople are motivated to work harder as they get closer to reaching their goals or quotas. Consequently, salespeople and managers need to know how they are progressing. At the same time, they can benefit from ongoing insights about effective strategies for achieving and exceeding their goals. Any sales compensation plan will have greater motivational impact when it's continually reinforced through feedback to the sales force.

Today's Information Technology Enables Powerful Feedback

More than ever, information technology is giving companies high-impact ways to share feedback with salespeople and managers. The proliferation of mobile devices makes it possible to reach salespeople and managers anywhere and anytime with information about their performance and what they need to do to achieve the next milestone. By layering analytics seamlessly on top of data, companies can deliver motivating feedback to sales force members while tailoring and targeting that information to the specific context a salesperson or manager faces.

Using Customized Feedback to Motivate Insurance Agents

A major insurance company wanted to do a better job of engaging new agents in selling. The company recruited tens of thousands of sales agents every year, and history had proved that agents who got off to a good start had a much better chance of staying with the company long term. Regrettably, too often new agents received inconsistent training, development and communication from headquarters. This dampened new agent motivation, led to considerable turnover of agents within their first year and hurt overall sales force productivity.

To help engage new agents, the company offered bonuses linked to the achievement of specific early performance milestones – for example, an early success bonus for achieving a certain sales level within the first month on the job. New agents could track their progress toward milestones at any time by logging in to the company's intranet and pulling down sales information. Unfortunately, the process of getting this information was cumbersome; many new agents didn't take the time to do it. Because these agents didn't know exactly where they stood, the motivational power of the bonus was limited.

The company conducted an experiment to test the motivational impact of more customized and timely performance feedback. The company selected a test group of new agents and pushed email information out to the agents in this group who were making good progress toward achieving milestones. The emails reported real-time progress and reminded agents about the bonus opportunity.

Messages were customized to each individual on the basis of time in the job and performance. For example, agents two weeks into the job who had achieved between 40% and 80% of the first-month milestone received a message encouraging them to continue to push hard to become eligible for the bonus by the end of the month. Agents who were already more than 80% of the way to the milestone at the two-week point received a different message, congratulating them on their outstanding performance and encouraging them to keep up the good work. The emails made data readily available to the agents and their managers, rather than requiring them to seek out the information themselves.

To measure the impact of the emails on new agent performance, the company compared the first-month performance of agents in the test group with that of agents in a control group (agents who were demographically similar to the test group but who did not receive emails).

The results are summarized in Figure 8-1. In the test group, 62% of the agents who had achieved between 40% and 80% of the early success sales milestone within their first two weeks (and who therefore received an encouragement email) exceeded the milestone and received a bonus at the end of the month.

In the control group, performance was less impressive. Only 54% of the agents who had achieved between 40% and 80% of the early success milestone within two weeks exceeded the milestone and received a bonus. This difference was statistically significant. The company attributed the performance gap to the reinforcing email message the agents in the test group received.

On the basis of these results, the company expanded the program to include many more new agents. The company also implemented additional email programs to enhance the motivational power of sales contests and other incentives for new and seasoned sales agents alike.

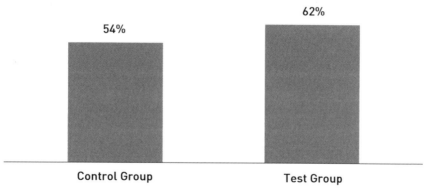

Figure 8-1. Percentage of Agents Qualifying for an Early Success Bonus

Additional Reading

The following sources offer more ideas about how information systems and analytics can provide salespeople and managers with feedback that enhances the motivational power of sales compensation:

- *The Future of Sales Compensation* (Albrecht and Marley)[2] provides insights about how to leverage technological advances to drive superior performance in your sales force, including ways to use gamification to encourage salespeople to modify their sales activity and boost performance.

- *The Power of Sales Analytics* (Zoltners, Sinha and Lorimer)[3] includes more examples of ways companies are boosting sales force performance (through incentives and other sales force programs) by getting the right information to the right people at the right time using the right medium.

Plan Health Checks to Help Leaders Make Course Corrections

In addition to increasing the motivational power of sales compensation, the right data, analytics and processes can help sales and compensation leaders identify potential problems and opportunities with a sales compensation plan. Routine plan health checks allow leaders to stay on top of plan performance, identify issues early and make modifications to drive continual improvement.

It's not enough to design a great sales compensation plan and then "set and forget" it. Especially in dynamic sales environments, the way the market evolves and the dynamics surrounding an incentive plan's impact on sales performance often turn out to be different from what sales leaders had expected. Consider some examples:

- **The national forecast is way off.** When a computer manufacturer launched a new line of products for the cloud computing market, executives set the national sales quota on the basis of overly optimistic expectations. Once salespeople figured out their quotas were unattainable, they stopped selling the products and focused on other products that were not as important to the company. This hurt the company's entry into this potentially lucrative market and made a bad situation even worse.

- **Company direction changes.** A computer products and services company that historically had sold direct to customers started using channel partners to reach more customers. The company adjusted the incentive plan so salespeople's credit for sales involving partners was 5% to 10% less, reflecting the partner's effort and commission. The company expected that partners would bring in many more sales and the increase in volume would more than make up for the reduced commission rate for salespeople. But salespeople lacked knowledge about how to work with partners and feared partner involvement in a sale would only negatively affect their earnings. The sales force failed to embrace the new indirect sales model.

- **Salespeople are gaming the plan.** A healthcare company paid salespeople a significant bonus for overachieving monthly quotas. Salespeople discovered they could make more money for less effort by making quota every other month. Some started managing the timing of their orders to optimize their earnings. As the end of the month approached, salespeople who felt they could not make this month's quota would delay placing orders until the following month, giving them a jump start on achieving next month's quota and earning the overachievement bonus that month. This behavior was not in the best interest of customers or the company. Figure 8-2 lists some other common undesired consequences of some incentive plan features.

Diagnostics to Help You Stay the Course

Companies can use many different types of analytics as part of a health check for determining whether the sales compensation plan is driving the desired behaviors and contributing to sales force performance. Here, we highlight several examples.

Is the Sales Compensation Plan Fair?

Plan fairness is important for motivation. Salespeople should have a fair opportunity to succeed, despite territory differences. For example, it should not be easier for a salesperson assigned to a territory with large market opportunity to make more money than it is for a salesperson who is assigned to a territory with smaller market opportunity. Other factors outside salespeople's control that affect performance include past performance (such as starting sales volume or market share) and the

Incentive Feature	Unwanted Behavior
Monthly overachievement bonus	➤ Sell every other month
Pay on customer satisfaction	➤ Seek satisfaction instead of sales
Pay on share	➤ Shrink territory
Pay on sales volume	➤ Enlarge territory
Team incentive	➤ Relax
Caps	➤ Hoard sales
Complex plan	➤ Ignore it
Manager determines reward	➤ Work the manager, not the customer
Very high incentive component	➤ Sell at all costs, invent applications
Paid on unit volume	➤ Discount

Figure 8-2. Some Undesired Consequences of Incentive Plan Features

level of challenge in the territory's quota (such as required sales growth). A high correlation between pay and any factor other than a salesperson's own effort and ability can reveal a bias in the compensation plan or in the quotas that underlie the plan.

At a pharmaceutical company, many salespeople felt that sales quotas were unfair, and this lowered motivation in a good portion of the sales team. The company conducted the fairness diagnostic test summarized in Figure 8-3. This involved checking to see if quota attainment was affected by external territory factors salespeople couldn't control.

External Factors	——— Average Quota Attainment ———		
	Top 30% of Salespeople	Middle 40% of Salespeople	Bottom 30% of Salespeople
Starting Sales Volume	101%	100%	98%
Starting Market Share	102%	101%	95%
Required Sales Growth	95%	100%	104%
Market Opportunity	98%	100%	101%

Figure 8-3. Diagnostic Test for Sales Compensation Plan Bias Based on Factors Salespeople Can't Control

In a fair plan with fair quotas, average quota attainment will be roughly the same across the top, middle and bottom groups for every external factor. A clear and pronounced trend in quota attainment across the groups for any factor may indicate unfairness. At the pharmaceutical company, the sales compensation plan may be unfair to salespeople who start with a low market share or who have a quota requiring high growth.

After seeing the diagnostic test results, the company revised its quota-setting formula so salespeople who had low starting market share in their territory were no longer penalized with quotas requiring unreasonably high growth expectations. The quotas for these salespeople still required growth beyond what was required in high-share territories, but the growth expectation was less extreme. Instead, a larger portion of the overall growth expectation was allocated to salespeople who had already built moderate market share in their territory, which accelerated their immediate growth opportunity. This improved the fairness of quotas and drove overall sales growth.

Is the Sales Compensation Plan Aligned With Strategy?

An effective sales compensation plan not only motivates a high quantity and quality of sales effort but also aligns sales effort with company goals and strategies. Looking at performance by product or customer group (in addition to looking at aggregate performance) can create insights about the extent to which a plan motivates sales effort aligned with company priorities.

A computer manufacturer uncovered an issue and remedied a potential problem by tracking incentive plan *engagement* by product, as shown in Figure 8-4. Engagement in the context of incentive plans is defined as the percentage of salespeople who have hit the minimum threshold to earn incentives (for the computer manufacturer, that threshold was 75% of quota for key products). The goal was for at least two-thirds of salespeople to be engaged on each product. Although overall compensation costs were tracking as planned, engagement for two products fell short of this goal. For one strategically important product (servers), engagement was only 43%; the majority of salespeople were earning no incentive pay at all for the product. The company investigated and discovered salespeople lacked confidence in selling the new product. By improving product training, coaching and sales materials, and introducing a fourth-quarter SPIFF, the company was able to re-engage the sales force and boost server sales.

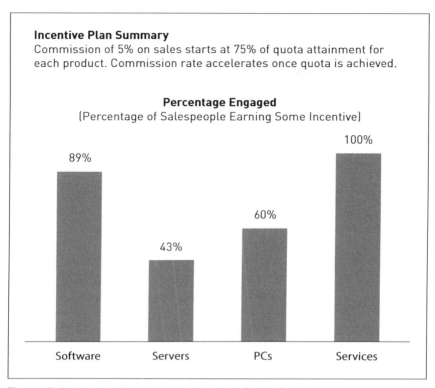

Incentive Plan Summary
Commission of 5% on sales starts at 75% of quota attainment for each product. Commission rate accelerates once quota is achieved.

Percentage Engaged
(Percentage of Salespeople Earning Some Incentive)

Figure 8-4. Analysis Showing Lack of Sales Force Engagement on Some Important Products

Is the Sales Compensation Plan Achieving the Desired Objectives?

A sales compensation plan health check can include a regularly produced scorecard tracking metrics that reflect the achievement of key compensation plan objectives. The scorecard in Figure 8-5 tracks metrics showing the extent to which the sales compensation plan is achieving three key objectives: paying for performance, being fiscally responsible and motivating the sales team. By tracking these metrics and comparing performance with benchmark ranges developed from historical norms and industry averages, the company identified performance gaps and course corrections needed to keep the sales force on track. In this case, there was concern the plan was not paying sufficiently for performance. With the 90th percentile earning less than the benchmark multiple of target pay and the 10th percentile earning more than the benchmark, the company looked to adjust the incentive plan so that more money went to top performers.

Objective	Plan Performance Metric	Benchmark	Actual	In Range?
Pays for Performance	Actual pay as a percentage of target pay for 10th percentile	10%–30%	38%	No
	Actual pay as a percentage of target pay for 90th percentile	200%–300%	190%	No
Is Fiscally Responsible	Actual pay as a percentage of target pay for all salespeople	100%–110%	100%	Yes
	Actual pay as a percentage of target pay for the 50th percentile (Median percentage of target pay)	100%	94%	No
Is Motivating	Engagement rate (Percentage earning some incentive pay)	90%–100%	96%	Yes
	Meaningful engagement rate (Percentage earning at least 75% of target incentive pay)	60%–80%	72%	Yes

Figure 8-5. Scorecard for Tracking Key Sales Compensation Plan Performance Metrics

Using Health Check Analytics to Evaluate Proposed Compensation Plans

The earlier examples of health check diagnostics demonstrate how companies use analytics *reactively* to understand how well the compensation plans currently in place have performed. Such backward-facing evaluations can provide insights about how to change current compensation plans to perform better in the future.

Health check diagnostics can also be used in another way – to allow companies *proactively* to test how well a proposed new compensation plan is likely to perform, before that plan is actually implemented. Prior to rolling out a new compensation plan, leaders will want to know: Will the new plan be fair? Will it align with strategy? Will it pay for performance? By evaluating a new plan design by using historical territory performance data, it's possible to get insights for answering these questions.

To do the evaluation, start with last year's territory performance data and calculate how much each salesperson would have earned had the new plan been in place. Then perform the health check analytics described earlier. If you discover any potential problems, you can change the plan design and re-evaluate repeatedly, until you feel the plan is ready to implement.

Using health check analytics for proactive plan testing can be complex and difficult work. For a more detailed description of the analytics required, see *The Complete Guide to Sales Force Incentive Compensation* (Zoltners, Sinha and Lorimer)[4] and *The Future of Sales Compensation* (Albrecht and Marley).[5]

Analyzing the Health of Your Sales Compensation Plan

Diagnostics and metrics, such as in the examples just given, can have value as stand-alone analyses prepared to address specific sales force issues or concerns. However, there is also great value in conducting sales compensation plan health checks on a regular basis. Many of the outputs can be produced through the sales compensation plan administration process. By making diagnosis of compensation plan health an ongoing process, as shown in Figure 8-6, companies can be more proactive in driving continuous sales force compensation plan improvement, especially in dynamic sales environments.

The steps required to implement a sales compensation plan health check process are described here.

Step 1: Develop a List of Objectives and Questions

First, with the input of sales and compensation leaders, identify the key objectives of your sales compensation plan and the questions for defining success in meeting those objectives. Examples include:

- Is the sales force on track to meet financial goals?
- How is performance trending over time, and do we need to make any changes?
- Is the plan working as intended? Does it motivate? Is it fair? Does it align with strategy? Does it pay for performance?

Step 2: Identify Metrics and Diagnostics

Next, identify the analytics that will help you answer the questions. Analytics may include a set of metrics (quantifiable measures) for tracking

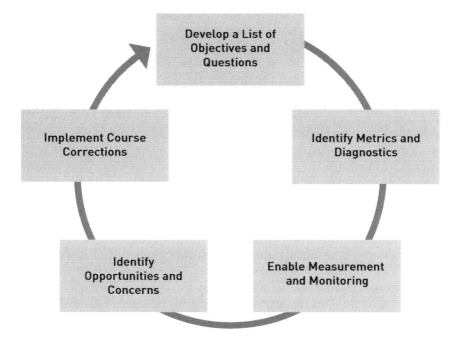

Figure 8-6. Sales Compensation Plan Health Check Process

compensation plan performance against objectives; Figure 8-5 provides an example. Analytics may also include diagnostics (tests for identifying specific compensation plan opportunities or problems) such as those shown in Figure 8-3. Metrics and diagnostics do not need to be complex to have impact, but it is necessary to have accurate and timely data at a sufficient level of detail.

In addition to the metrics and diagnostics suggested in this chapter, some other references to help you identify useful analytics are:

- *The Future of Sales Compensation* (Albrecht and Marley)[6] provides advice and examples of how to take your sales compensation analytics to the next level by using predictive analytics.
- *The Power of Sales Analytics* (Zoltners, Sinha and Lorimer)[7] provides many examples of analytics for gauging the impact of sales compensation as well as other sales force programs and decisions that can affect sales effectiveness.
- *The Complete Guide to Sales Force Incentive Compensation* (Zoltners, Sinha and Lorimer)[8] includes many detailed examples of analytics for evaluating the impact of current and new sales compensation plans.

Step 3: Enable Measurement and Monitoring

Put the systems and processes in place to track the metrics and diagnostics regularly. Quite often, the inputs required are already available or can easily be produced with existing sales compensation plan administration systems. Many systems allow real-time access to the latest data anytime and anywhere. However, it's not necessary to monitor constantly to have impact. Even monthly reporting can allow sales forces to identify and address many problems before they grow to crisis levels.

Step 4: Identify Opportunities and Concerns

Develop benchmarks or desired ranges for key metrics on the basis of historical performance, industry averages or best practice standards. Compare current performance with benchmarks, and monitor trends over time. The analysis shown in Figure 8-7 tracks two key pay-for-performance metrics for one sales force over a three-year period. If the current trend continues, these metrics will soon drift outside the company's target ranges for this sales force, indicating an issue that requires further investigation and perhaps remedial action.

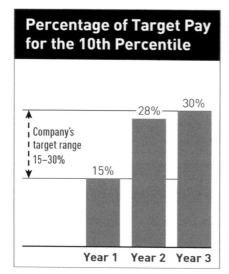 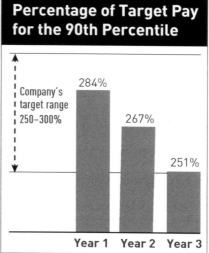

Figure 8-7. Analysis Tracking Pay-for-Performance Metrics in a Sales Force

Step 5: Implement Course Corrections

Take timely action as needed to address issues as they arise, and prevent bigger trouble down the road. Quite often, course corrections lead to refinement of the initial objectives and questions, making the health check process continuous and focused on bringing about ongoing sales force improvement in an ever-changing sales environment.

Conclusion

Using today's data, information systems and analytic capabilities, companies can provide more and higher-impact feedback to motivate salespeople and managers, while also better monitoring the performance of their sales compensation plans. Using analytics effectively to enhance the power of a current sales compensation plan is an underrealized opportunity for many sales forces. With all the data and analytics available today, there is great potential to enhance the impact of your sales compensation plan and ensure it consistently produces the best results.

Endnotes

1   Joseph C. Nunes and Xavier Drèze, "The Endowed Progress Effect: How Artificial Advancement Increases Effort," *Journal of Consumer Research,* March 2006, 504–12.

2   Chad Albrecht and Steve Marley, *The Future of Sales Compensation* (Evanston, IL: ZS Associates, Inc., 2016).

3   Andris A. Zoltners, Prabhakant Sinha and Sally E. Lorimer, *The Power of Sales Analytics* (Evanston, IL: ZS Associates, Inc., 2014).

4   Andris A. Zoltners, Prabhakant Sinha and Sally E. Lorimer, *The Complete Guide to Sales Force Incentive Compensation: How to Design and Implement Plans That Work* (New York: AMACOM, 2006).

5   Albrecht and Marley, *Sales Compensation.*

6   Ibid.

7   Zoltners, Sinha and Lorimer, *Sales Analytics.*

8   Zoltners, Sinha and Lorimer, *Incentive Compensation.*

SECTION 3

Addressing Perpetual Sales Compensation Issues

The final two chapters focus on sales compensation issues that for decades have been causing well-designed sales compensation plans to fail. The chapters provide readers with actionable ideas for addressing two perennial challenges.

Chapter 9   Setting Quotas That Motivate

Understand how analytics and a defined process can help you address the challenge of setting effective sales force quotas.

Chapter 10   Helping the Sales Force Embrace Compensation Plan Change

Learn proactive strategies that will increase sales force commitment to sales compensation plan change.

CHAPTER 9

Setting Quotas That Motivate

Understanding the Quota-Setting Challenge

According to the Incentive Practices Research (IPR) study[1] that ZS conducts every year, more than 80% of companies across industries set territory quotas. Very often, companies link incentive payout to quota performance, meaning that the incentive plan for these companies is only as good as the quotas that are set. Quota setting has been the number one compensation design issue selected by companies participating in the survey, across all industries, for three years straight, and it has been among the top three issues since 2007.

Simply put, setting quotas is a huge challenge for most sales forces. Because the vast majority of sales incentive compensation plans link pay to quota attainment, good quotas are essential for an incentive program that is both motivating and fiscally responsible.

Why You Need a Process for Setting Good Quotas

Consider the quota-setting dynamics shown in Figure 9-1. An appropriate sales quota is one that falls in a range of good to peak effort. This ideal range provides reasonable but not unrealistic stretch and leads to top sales effort and the highest performance.

Too often, quotas fall outside of the ideal range. If a salesperson gets a quota that is too low, that salesperson is overpaid. Far more often, a salesperson gets a quota that is too high, with so much stretch that the salesperson views the quota as unachievable. The salesperson loses motivation, and sales come in even lower than they would have had

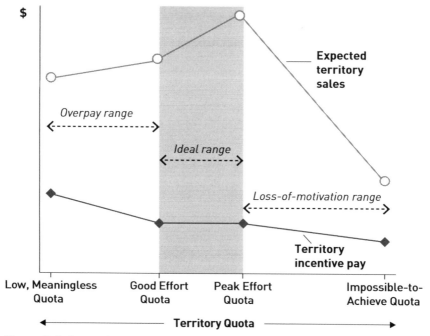

Figure 9-1. Quota-Setting Dynamics

the quota been set at a reasonable level. Once you get beyond the ideal range, a higher sales quota leads to lower sales.

A good quota-setting process consistently creates quotas that encourage peak sales effort for all salespeople, leading to strong financial results.

Characteristics of Good Quotas

Good quotas have the following characteristics:

- **Reasonable:** The quotas reflect market realities and provide an accurate estimate of what is possible. The quotas are challenging yet achievable.

- **Fair:** All salespeople have similar opportunity to achieve their quota, despite differences in territory opportunity. All salespeople have equally challenging quotas.

- **Simple to understand:** Salespeople should believe that the factors and calculations that determined their quota are logical so that they can commit to their quota.

- **Easy to administer:** Good quotas are enabled by accurate data, appropriate systems and streamlined processes.

Creating quotas that meet all of these criteria is possible but is extremely difficult to do.

Signs of a Quota-Setting Problem

Some *possible* indicators of a quota-setting issue include the following:

- Too many salespeople are extreme outliers in terms of quota performance – on either the high or the low end of the spectrum.
- Spending on sales incentive compensation is higher than expected.
- There is significant variation in salesperson rankings on quota attainment from year to year.
- The percentage of salespeople who make quota is substantially higher than the percentage your company targets.
- The percentage of salespeople who miss quota is substantially higher than the percentage your company targets.
- Turnover of good salespeople is higher than industry norms.

What Can Go Wrong With Quotas

When things go awry with quotas, it's for one or more of the following reasons.

The Overall Company Goal Is Too High

When 25% of salespeople miss quota, there may be a problem with those salespeople. However, when the majority of salespeople miss quota, the problem is most likely that the overall company goal is too high. With an overly aggressive company goal, quotas are consistently too high across the sales force. The result is a dispirited sales team, suboptimal sales and high sales force turnover.

The following are frequent reasons that a company sales goal is too high:

- **Unanticipated market dynamics:** Consider what happened at a financial services company. Executives set the annual company sales goal in a booming economy. When a second-quarter recession hit, it became evident that sales force quotas were unrealistic. By the end of August, fewer than 10% of salespeople had any chance of making quota. Salespeople became discouraged and angry that the company was treating them unfairly. Most disengaged and began holding sales for the following year, when they hoped that quotas would be attainable. Executives contemplated reducing quotas midstream to re-energize the sales force but feared this would compromise quota-setting integrity.

- **Overly ambitious company forecasts:** Consider the case of a computer manufacturer and one of its strategically important product lines. Executives formulated a company sales goal based on optimistic expectations and a desire to promise strong sales to the investment community, not on analysis of market realities. The goal was handed down to the sales force, and salespeople figured out quickly that their quotas were unattainable. They all but stopped selling the product line to focus on other product categories that had achievable quotas and enabled them to earn more money. The error hurt the company's share of an important market.

- **Systematic padding:** This situation may begin with an accurate company goal, but in the end, the quotas allocated down to salespeople are systematically too high. At a professional services firm, the vice president of sales added 5% onto the company goal to ensure a safe cushion before passing it down to the regional level. The regional directors tacked on another 5% before allocating quotas to the district managers, who added their own 5% safety net. By the time the process got down to salespeople, territory quotas summed to more than 15% above the original company goal. Salespeople perceived the quotas to be unrealistic, and only 30% hit their individual number, yet at the national sales meeting, the vice president congratulated the team for hitting the overall number. The situation frustrated the sales force, many top performers left to join rival companies, and the vice president was gone within two years.

The Overall Company Goal Is Too Low

This happens less frequently than the problem of an overly challenging company goal, but when it does happen, sales force performance can suffer. Generally, when an overall company goal is too low, it's because leaders must make their forecasts in the face of uncertain market conditions. Underforecasting of company sales leads to quotas that are consistently too low across the sales force. The result is an unchallenged sales team, suboptimal sales and overly generous incentive payouts.

The following are frequent reasons that a company sales goal is too low:

- **Unanticipated market dynamics:** When a large industrial products company underforecasted market demand for its products, it set territory quotas that were uniformly too easily achieved. The vast majority of salespeople reached their quota by midyear. Even though company leaders were pleased that sales exceeded expectations, the forecasting error hurt the company in three ways. First, annual incentive costs were much higher than budgeted because the company had to pay salespeople a lot of money for only moderate work effort. Second, as the year-end approached, some salespeople started to delay closing deals in order to have them count toward next year's quota, which they knew would be more challenging. Third, the mistake had an undesirable impact on future sales force expectations. Some salespeople felt that they were entitled to continued high pay for moderate work, making it difficult for the company to set more challenging quotas for the following year without adversely affecting morale.

- **Conservative budgeting:** When sales leaders are asked to weigh in on the appropriate company goal, it's in their best interest to err on the side of making the goal too low. It's easier to motivate the sales force when the majority of salespeople believe they can make quota; in fact, some sales leaders follow a rule of thumb that suggests 75% should hit quota. With reasonable quotas, the majority of salespeople will feel successful, and the sales force is assured of beating the goal and making more money. At one large pharmaceutical company, marketing forecasters set what appeared to be an aggressive annual goal for the following year. The goal called for accelerating sales growth well beyond historical trends. Sales leaders were able to convince top management to reduce the goal by arguing that because the goal deviated significantly from the historical trend, it must be unrealistic and unobtainable. In the end, actual sales came in very close to marketing's original forecast. The sales force had "overachieved" the reduced goal, and salespeople earned more money than they otherwise would have.

The Overall Company Goal Is Misallocated Among Salespeople

Even when companies set a reasonable overall company goal, there can be problems with quotas at the individual salesperson level. If the reasonable company goal isn't allocated appropriately among salespeople, an individual's quota that is too low is offset by someone else's quota that is too high. Some salespeople get quotas that are too easy to reach, while others get quotas that are impossible to achieve. The result: discontent among salespeople about quota fairness and a measurably negative impact on profitability. The profit reduction is a result of two dynamics. First, there is a loss of sales in territories with quotas that are too high because salespeople are in the loss-of-motivation range shown in Figure 9-1. Second, there are excessive costs in territories with quotas that are too low because salespeople are in the overpay range shown in Figure 9-1.

Companies may misallocate the company sales goal for the following reasons:

- **The quota allocation formula doesn't acknowledge factors that a salesperson can't control.** Frequently, this happens because territory opportunity is not taken into account in the quota-setting formula. One healthcare company set a challenging yet reasonable company goal of 20% sales growth and gave each salesperson a quota equal to 120% of the amount he or she sold the previous year. Top salespeople felt the quotas were unfair. "I had a great year, so they 'rewarded' me with an even tougher quota, even though I've already captured most of my territory's potential." The discontent of top performers was exacerbated when they saw that their peers with a lower sales base (and therefore lower quotas) were exceeding quotas easily without working particularly hard. Top performers reasoned, "I'm not going to make quota this year, so the best strategy is to hold back so I get a low quota next year." An allocation that failed to acknowledge differences in territory opportunity created this hero-to-zero situation. The unintentional stretch in the quotas for the company's best performers alienated this critical group.

- **Managers assign quotas using challenge-the-stars logic.** When sales managers have input as to how the quota for their region should be allocated among salespeople, a common strategy is to give a disproportionately large share of the region's quota to the strongest salespeople – the ones the manager can rely on to deliver. This strategy can work for a short time, but if used consistently, the result can be the same as in the prior case in which the formula didn't acknowledge differences in territory opportunity – weak performers get easier quotas, and the best salespeople are not rewarded enough for their hard work and superior results. Strong performers observe poor performers making more money for less work, and the impact on morale can be devastating.

Three Ways to Improve Quota Setting

Fortunately, advances in data and information systems today are opening up new possibilities to improve territory quota setting. There are three keys to make your quota-setting process more effective.

Acknowledge Territory Opportunity When Setting Quotas

Territory market opportunity is measured by factors such as the number and size of customers and prospects, growth potential of the market, the degree of competitive intensity and other factors that are outside of the sales force's control yet influence a salesperson's chance of making sales. If you fail to acknowledge differences in market opportunity from territory to territory, quotas are very likely to be unfair. This error is easy to make and is especially costly because it often punishes your top performers. Salespeople who achieve high sales and high levels of market penetration are "rewarded" with tougher quotas every year; at some point, these quotas become nearly impossible to achieve because so much of the territories' opportunity has already been captured.

By incorporating data that capture an accurate measure of territory market opportunity in the quota-setting process, you increase quota fairness. Good measures of territory opportunity also allow you to create better metrics that reflect salespeople's true performance.

In some industries, measures of market opportunity are readily available. In industries such as airlines and pharmaceuticals, data companies sell information on sales of all competitive products by account or local market. In other industries, creative approaches are required to develop good surrogate measures.

A telecom company developed a collaborative filtering model, similar in concept to algorithms used by companies such as Netflix and Amazon, to forecast the size of the opportunity and the likelihood of purchase at each account. The model suggested which products and services each customer might buy on the basis of analysis of past purchases within that account, as well as purchases in other accounts with a similar profile. In addition to measuring market opportunity, the data helped salespeople present the right products to the right customers, driving stronger uptake of new products and improving the realization of cross-selling and up-selling opportunities.

It's not always necessary to use complex analytics to estimate market opportunity. A greeting card company used U.S. Census Bureau data to estimate the opportunity at retail stores by looking at population and average household income within a three-mile radius of each store. A company that sold insurance and financing as part of a bundled service offering on retail sales of motorcycles used customer demographic characteristics, competitors, the presence of local credit unions and the onset of spring weather (which triggered an increase in motorcycle sales) to predict territory opportunity. Imperfect but directionally correct estimates of market opportunity are better than no estimates at all and can allow you to improve the accuracy and fairness of quotas significantly.

Use Rigorous Analytics When Setting Quotas

Many companies, because of either lack of time or lack of expertise, fail to apply the necessary analytic rigor to setting territory quotas. The best companies not only use analytics to set quotas but also test quotas for their likely impact on sales and profits *before* handing quotas out to the sales force.

Analytics for Setting Quotas

Using data-driven formulas as part of the quota-setting process generally leads to territory quotas that are more objective and fair. There are many possible quota-setting formulas and analytic approaches. A useful reference describing many such approaches is *The Complete Guide to Sales Force Incentive Compensation* (Zoltners, Sinha and Lorimer).[2]

When considering the type of formula to use, take into account your company's selling situation, analytical capabilities and data availability. There is usually a trade-off between simplicity and accuracy. A complex formula that creates very realistic quotas can be difficult and costly to implement. A complex formula can also be hard to explain to the sales force, although the need for explanation depends largely on the sales culture. Some sales forces expect salespeople to accept quotas without much justification; others feel the need for greater transparency. Sometimes a simpler process, though less exact, creates a better result because the sales force will more readily understand and embrace the quotas.

The two examples shown in the following inset boxes describe analytically based quota-setting approaches that create a good balance of analytics for accuracy and simplicity and for gaining sales force understanding and commitment.

Maintenance Plus Adjusted Growth Method of Setting Territory Quotas

The maintenance plus adjusted growth method illustrated in Figure 9-2 results in a quota for each salesperson that has two components: maintenance and growth.

The approach illustrated in the example requires historical territory-level sales and market opportunity data. The *maintenance* portion of the quota asks each salesperson to retain 100% of last year's territory sales. The *growth* portion of the quota requires salespeople to grow territory sales in proportion to the market opportunity in their territory. For example, if a territory has 2% of the national market opportunity, that territory gets a growth quota equal to 2% of the national quota gap (the national quota for this year minus last year's national sales). The growth quota will be a larger proportion of the overall quota in a territory that has large market opportunity and a smaller proportion of the overall quota in a territory that has low market opportunity.

Companies can use different approaches for calculating both the maintenance and the growth portions of quotas. In some market conditions, it's appropriate to give salespeople maintenance quotas equal to more than 100% of last year's sales – such as when markets are growing or have high repeat sales. In other market conditions, a percentage of less than 100% of last year's sales is appropriate – such as when markets are relatively flat or declining or have low repeat sales. There are also different ways to calculate the growth portion of the quota. Some companies ask everyone to grow sales by the same amount, especially during a new product launch before the company has enough data to determine territory opportunity.

The maintenance plus growth method of quota setting can produce good results in terms of quota accuracy and fairness and, at the same time, is fairly easy to implement and explain to the sales force.

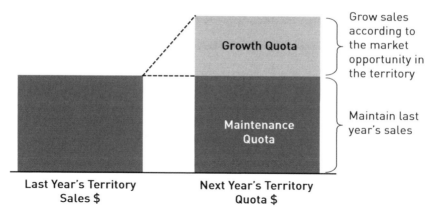

Figure 9-2. Maintenance Plus Adjusted Growth Method of Setting Quotas

Weighted Index Method of Setting Territory Quotas

The weighted index method shown in Figure 9-3 is a good method for setting quotas based on multiple factors that can influence territory sales. The method can be useful in the early stages of a product's life cycle, when there is limited sales history available and many factors are believed to affect sales.

The approach requires territory-level data about key factors that influence territory sales. These can include unrealized market opportunity, market growth, previous period sales, sales growth, key customer penetration, customer demographic characteristics, land area, local regulations, competitor presence and other relevant factors. For purposes of illustration, the example uses just two factors – previous period sales and untapped market sales. Each factor gets a weighting that reflects its importance in influencing sales opportunity, with the factors and their weightings determined using analytics (such as regression models) and management input. Each territory gets a percentage of the national sales quota that equals the weighted sum of that territory's percentage of the nation across all of the factors.

The weighted index method enables reasonable and fair quotas by acknowledging many differences across territories. Because many factors can be considered, salespeople are likely to feel that the quota allocation process is fair and unbiased, and the impact of data errors in any one factor is reduced.

	Previous Period Sales History			Untapped Market Sales			Quota
	Sales ($ Millions)	Percentage of the Nation	Portion of National Goal ($ Millions)	Untapped Market Sales ($ Millions)	Percentage of the Nation	Portion of National Goal ($ Millions)	($ Millions)
Territory A	1.3	14%	1.4	9.2	10%	1.0	1.2
Territory B	2.6	29%	2.9	23.6	26%	2.6	2.7
Territory C	5.2	57%	5.7	59.2	64%	6.4	6.1
Nation	9.1	100%	10.0	92.0	100%	10.0	10.0
Weighting		40%			60%		

Territory A Sales Quota = 40% × $1.4 + 60% × $1.0 = $1.2 Million

Figure 9-3. Weighted Index Method of Setting Territory Quotas

Analytics for Evaluating Quotas

Analytics are also useful for evaluating quotas for characteristics such as reasonableness and fairness. By evaluating quotas at the end of every incentive period, you can find out whether your quotas are producing the desired results and whether you need to make any adjustments to the quota-setting approach before the next period. You can also use analytics to test a proposed quota-setting method before implementing it so you can anticipate problems and make appropriate adjustments to your method before handing quotas out to the sales force.

Consider two examples of useful analytics for evaluating quotas:

First, you can test quotas for reasonableness by looking at the correlation between the quota and actual sales at the territory level. The expected degree of variability depends on the market and the product life cycle. The example in Figure 9-4 shows an amount of variability in quota attainment that is typical with a good quota-setting approach for a stable product and market; much more variability is expected with a newer product or market. Too much variability in quota attainment suggests a possible need to revisit the quota-setting method.

Second, you can test quotas for fairness by evaluating quota attainment for groups of territories with similar characteristics to look for historical

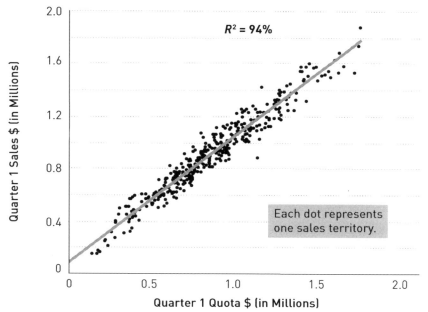

Figure 9-4. A Test for Reasonableness in Quota Setting

biases. The analysis in Figure 9-5 shows the range of quota attainment for the middle 50% of territories (the 25th to the 75th percentile) in three groups of territories at one company – those with low, medium and high sales growth in the previous year. The analysis revealed a bias in the quota-setting formula. Territories with historically low sales growth received quotas that were too easily achieved, and territories with historically high growth received quotas that were too challenging. This information prompted the company to change its quota-setting method. Instead of basing quotas mostly on historical growth trends in each territory, the company began to factor unrealized market opportunity into the quota-setting formula. The result was fairer quotas for everyone, leading to more consistent quota achievement across the three groups.

Bias testing can compare quota attainment across territories grouped according to many different factors – historical sales or growth, market size or growth, starting market share, the number and types of accounts in the territory. A correlation between quota attainment and any factor outside of a salesperson's control can suggest a possible bias in the quota-allocation process.

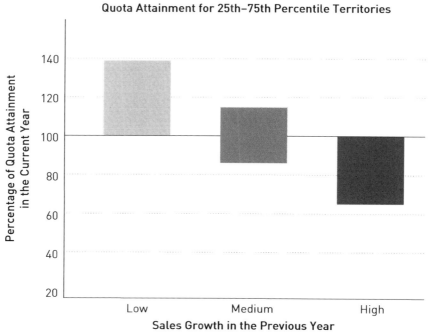

Figure 9-5. A Test for Quota Bias Based on Previous Year Growth

Incentive Plan Designs That Acknowledge Quota-Setting Uncertainties

In unpredictable selling environments (a volatile economy, a first-of-a-kind product), even the best forecasting techniques, data and quota-setting methods cannot overcome the uncertainty inherent in predicting sales. Several incentive plan design strategies for uncertain environments can help you ensure that sales force motivation stays high (if quotas are too high) and undeserved incentive payouts are minimized (if quotas are too low).

- **Set quotas that reward a realistic range of performance.** Rather than setting quotas that focus sales force attention on a single number, define different performance ranges for salespeople to aim for. For example, define a success range of quota attainment that begins at 80% of the target sales level. This helps more salespeople feel successful, even if their quota comes to be seen as unrealistically high. The percentage of quota attainment at which payout begins should be lower the more uncertain your forecast and the wider the expected range of quota attainment across salespeople.

- **Set quotas with short time frames.** If quotas turn out to be unreasonable, the sales force is affected only for a limited time, and the impact of the error is minimized. However, there is a flip side: A shorter time frame produces more variability in performance, and a longer time frame provides more opportunity for variability to average out.

- **Use earnings caps or decelerators.** Although such features can dampen the motivation of top performers, caps and decelerators can be justified in unpredictable environments to protect the company against excessive incentive costs if quotas are set too low. Consider offering a special reward outside the main incentive plan to a top performer who gets penalized by a cap or decelerator and who truly deserves the reward.

- **Design payout curves that adjust with company quota attainment.** Link an individual's incentive payout to his or her own territory quota performance and also to quota performance across the rest of the sales force. For example, if the salesperson achieves 100% of his or her territory quota, the salesperson earns the target incentive amount if company quota attainment is also 100%. The salesperson earns more than target if company quota attainment is below 100%, reflecting the fact that the salesperson outperformed average sales force performance. The salesperson earns less than target if company attainment is above 100%, acknowledging his or her underperformance relative to others.

These incentive plan design features help you manage sales force motivation and incentive compensation costs when accurate quota setting is made difficult by an unpredictable environment.

Give Sales Managers an Opportunity to Refine Quotas

Enhance the quality of territory quotas by engaging sales managers in the quota-setting process. Local knowledge allows managers to refine quotas to reflect on-the-ground realities not recognized in quotas that are set based on data alone. In addition, participation by sales managers in the quota-setting process increases their commitment to quotas and enables them to sell those quotas more effectively to the salespeople they manage.

An efficient and effective quota-refinement process allows sales managers to make zero-sum adjustments to preliminary analytically calculated territory sales quotas. With the right information and online tools, sales managers can review and adjust quotas easily, with reasonable limits on the degree of change allowed. Managers can submit changes to headquarters for review and approval and can document and accurately communicate quota adjustments. The inset box describes the rigorous process that one pharmaceutical company uses to engage sales managers in the quota-refinement process.

A Sales Force Quota-Refinement Process

A pharmaceutical sales force organized into multiple management levels – regions, districts and territories – uses a down-and-up approach to set sales force quotas. The approach involves the following steps:

1. **Set regional quotas.**
   a. Allocate the national quota to the territory level by using a prescribed, data-based formula. Roll the territory quotas up to the regional level to produce preliminary regional quotas.
   b. Get input from the national sales vice president about regional quotas. Allow adjustments if the vice president feels that the

formula has overlooked important regional factors. By using web-based software to track adjustments, the company can easily ensure that adjusted regional quotas still sum to the national quota.

2. **Set district quotas.**
   a. Cascade each region's adjusted quota to the territories in the region by using the prescribed formula. Roll the territory quotas up to the district level to produce preliminary district quotas.
   b. Get input from regional directors about the district-level quotas. Allow directors to make changes if they feel the formula has overlooked important district factors. Changes to district quotas are subject to approval by the national sales vice president. Software ensures that the adjusted district quotas still sum to the regional quotas.

3. **Set territory quotas.**
   a. Cascade each district's adjusted quota to the territories in the district.
   b. Allow district managers to make adjustments to territory quotas if they feel the formula has overlooked important territory factors. Changes to territory quotas are subject to the approval of regional directors. Software ensures that the adjusted territory quotas still sum to the district quotas.

By using web-based software to administer the adjustment and review processes, the company gets quick turnaround, accuracy of adjustments and an audit trail of all changes. The back-and-forth approach provides the benefits of using a formula to set quotas and, at the same time, captures the local knowledge of regional directors and district managers. Sales directors and managers better understand how quotas are set and can more knowledgeably communicate them to salespeople, which increases the sales force's commitment to the quotas.

Conclusion

Sales force quota setting is a perpetual challenge for most companies, given forecasting uncertainties and diverse business conditions across local markets, yet getting quotas right is extremely important. The right quotas challenge salespeople to be the best that they can be and, thus, are a key tool for motivating salespeople to drive sales results.

A good quota-setting process produces fair and reasonable quotas that acknowledge differences in market opportunity across territories. The best processes use analytics to set quotas and evaluate them for qualities such as reasonableness and fairness. The best processes also incorporate sales force input so that analytically based quotas reflect local knowledge and have the commitment of the sales team.

With the right quota-setting process in place, you can consistently set quotas that lead to peak sales force effort and produce strong company financial results.

Endnotes

1   ZS Incentive Practices Research (IPR) study. Data are gathered annually through a survey of sales compensation professionals in multiple industries worldwide. Results are provided to participating companies.

2   Andris A. Zoltners, Prabhakant Sinha and Sally E. Lorimer, *The Complete Guide to Sales Force Incentive Compensation: How to Design and Implement Plans That Work* (New York: AMACOM, 2006).

CHAPTER 10

Helping the Sales Force Embrace Compensation Plan Change

Implementing Change in Today's Sales Environment

When companies make changes to sales compensation and incentive plans, they typically spend at least 80% of their time designing the plan. This includes activities such as understanding the sales strategy, collecting data, interviewing plan participants and sales leaders, crafting plan design alternatives, modeling likely outcomes and selecting the best plan. That leaves less than 20% of time for implementation. Implementing a plan involves developing transition strategies and communication and training documents needed to roll out the plan to the sales force. It also involves executing a process for engaging the sales force in understanding and embracing the change.

Although a 20% focus on implementation may be sufficient for minor plan tweaks, it is inadequate when the change is significant. Perhaps this lack of attention to implementation explains why sales compensation professionals so often tell us one of their biggest challenges is the failure of salespeople to understand a sales incentive plan (even a relatively simple one). Beyond understanding a new plan, salespeople also need to accept and embrace the change for the plan to have the desired impact.

Forces of change in today's sales environment are creating a need for some companies to transform their sales forces. This creates anxieties that can make winning the hearts and minds of salespeople very difficult when implementing incentive plan change. Salespeople may already feel on the defensive with the many changes management is imposing on them. These include changes such as the following:

- creating less expensive sales roles, while reducing the number of people in traditional field sales positions as more selling shifts to inside sales and online channels

- redesigning many sales force programs, including sales compensation, as generational diversity increasingly affects the workplace

- implementing new performance metrics and payout formulas that focus on profitability and potentially change the income opportunity for salespeople

- rolling out initiatives aimed at enhancing the effectiveness of salespeople around the world, including globalized sales incentive compensation programs

- introducing new technologies and data to enhance selling, while requiring salespeople to develop new skills and adapt to new work processes

When implementing major changes such as these, the effort that goes into making sure the sales force understands and believes in the change can be just as important as the design of the change itself. Effective implementation requires sales force involvement and focus on change management throughout the entire project. With compensation plan change, attention to change management should start when you diagnose the current incentive plan, should continue throughout the new plan design phase and should increase in importance as you implement the new plan.

This chapter describes some circumstances that make major compensation and incentive plan change challenging. The chapter also discusses specific strategies for addressing difficult transitions and stresses the importance of change management for ensuring sales force understanding and acceptance of compensation and incentive plan change.

What Makes Change Challenging?

Assuming there are no legal barriers to implementing incentive plan change (for example, in Germany, work councils must approve sales compensation plan changes), a big part of what makes incentive plan change so challenging is the risk of losing salespeople and customers.

Situations That Create Risk of Losing Salespeople

Compensation and incentive plan change has a personal impact on every member of the sales force. Gaining understanding and acceptance of a major change can be very difficult. There is considerable risk of losing salespeople, especially if the labor market is strong and your competitors are poaching people. Gaining sales force acceptance, and thus holding on to your best people, will be more difficult in the following circumstances.

When the Sales Force Rarely Changes

For some sales forces, change is part of the culture. One pharmaceutical company implemented incentive plan and other sales force changes almost every year and frequently tweaked the incentive plan quarterly as markets and company strategies evolved and leaders sought to make ongoing improvements. Some sales forces rarely change. An industrial manufacturing company had the same sales compensation plan for more than 30 years, with salespeople earning 80% of their pay from a commission on total revenues. All other things being equal, the industrial manufacturer will have a harder time implementing incentive plan change than will the pharmaceutical company that already has a strong culture of change in place.

When No Big Event Drives the Change

Some sales compensation plan change comes about in response to major events occurring either externally in the marketplace (sudden economic decline, new competitors, new government regulations) or within the company (a product launch, a sales force restructure). New company leadership can also initiate sales compensation change, especially when new leaders seek to make a statement and change the sales culture. When these events occur, the sales force is likely to expect incentive plan change. Although some salespeople may be unhappy and apprehensive about the change, at least they can understand why it's happening.

Other compensation plan changes are evolutionary. There are no major changes to market dynamics or company strategies, yet things aren't working as expected. Certain products or markets aren't achieving their sales goals or getting enough sales force attention. Finance wants to improve the plan's ability to pay for performance and contain costs. Changing the plan under such circumstances creates a challenge because the sales force may not see the need for and benefits of making the change.

When There Is Considerable Income Redistribution

All sales force members dislike sales compensation plan changes that make a plan universally less attractive – for example, raising everyone's quota by 5% – but the dynamics of incentive plan change become more complex when a change significantly helps some salespeople and hurts others.

For example, a change in the plan structure (commission on all sales versus payout tied to quota attainment) or the pay mix (salary versus incentive) can result in redistribution of income across the sales force, especially if there are large differences in performance across salespeople or differences in sales potential across territories. Those who stand to gain as a result of the change are happy about the personal benefit, but those who stand to lose are unhappy about the income reduction and may perceive the plan change as unfair.

A Situation That Creates Risk of Losing Customers: When Salespeople Have Customer Power

Anytime you implement a sales compensation plan change that risks losing salespeople, you risk losing their customers as well. However, the risk of customer loss is especially high in situations in which salespeople have power over customer relationships.

Consider the case of a large financial service firm. Salespeople sold investment products to individuals of high net worth and for years had earned a commission on all the investments they sold. Many salespeople who had established relationships and built their book of business earned well more than $1 million a year while working only 30 hours a week.

Without asking the sales force for input, members of the firm's new executive team implemented a team-based sales structure designed to reduce the amount of power individual salespeople had to control customer relationships. At the same time, they cut commission rates in half. More than half of the sales force quit, taking business representing more than 60% of the firm's assets with them.

In sales forces in which individual salespeople who control customer relationships earn a large portion of their pay through incentives, major changes to the sales compensation plan can create significant sales force and customer disruption.

Addressing Challenging Incentive Plan Changes

Several strategies can help you gain sales force understanding and acceptance of difficult-to-implement compensation plan changes.

Changing the Pay Mix

Significant changes to the pay mix can be considered when a sales role change affects the degree of influence individual salespeople have over customer buying decisions. Today, team-based and multichannel selling are reducing some salespeople's impact on sales and making it difficult to measure individual results. One way to address this issue is to move to a larger salary portion of pay; another is to link incentives to team rather than individual performance. Few companies have implemented a pay mix shift yet, likely because they don't want to risk losing top performers to competitors that pay salespeople large incentives. Pay mix shifts in the other direction – to a larger incentive portion – can come about when a sales role change gives individual salespeople more measurable impact on buying decisions, such as when a sales role shifts from retaining customers to driving new sales.

Significant pay mix changes can also come about when a company's leaders (often a new management team) seek to transform the sales culture. It can be argued that a larger salary portion of pay reinforces a culture that is customer oriented and focused on providing service and solutions, while a larger incentive portion encourages a culture that is more sales oriented and entrepreneurial. Some key arguments for both cultures are summarized in Figure 10-1.

Anticipating the Sales Force's Reaction

A significant pay mix change in either direction is challenging to implement. People who want sales jobs that are mostly salary typically have a different personality profile and tolerance for risk than do the people who prefer sales jobs that are mostly incentive pay. Some typical characteristics of salespeople who prefer guaranteed salary (even if it means less upside opportunity) include being customer focused, problem solving, team oriented, interested in professional development and appreciative of direction from management about how to succeed. Some typical characteristics of salespeople who prefer incentives (and are willing to forgo income guarantees in exchange for the possibility of higher pay)

Benefits of a Culture Reinforced by a Larger Salary Component
• Encourages long-term customer focus and discourages behaviors not in the best interest of customers or the company • Aligns with the needs of today's better-informed customers • Allows other sales management tools (performance management, training, coaching, sales data and tools) to set the right tone and motivate and direct sales activity

Benefits of a Culture Reinforced by a Larger Incentive Component
• Motivates and energizes salespeople • Encourages salespeople to act in alignment with company goals while working without close supervision • Helps attract and retain achievement-oriented and risk-taking salespeople • Keeps sales force costs in line with revenues

Figure 10-1. Arguments for Two Alternative Sales Cultures and Pay Mixes

include being focused on short-term results, being competitive, being motivated by money and recognition and wanting to be empowered to make their own decisions. Usually, the preference for salary versus incentives is determined largely by a salesperson's innate personality and cannot be changed. Consequently, a significant shift in the pay mix can lead to substantial sales force turnover.

When contemplating a significant pay mix change, consider how different salespeople are likely to feel about the change. Will top performers and others important to the company's future success be helped or hurt by the change? Look at the personality characteristics and risk-taking tolerance of the salespeople you'd like to keep, develop strategies for addressing any unhappiness that might result (some specific strategies are discussed later) and anticipate how much sales force turnover to expect.

Implementing an Incentive Portion Increase

Gaining acceptance of an increase to the incentive portion of pay is easier when the perception (or reality) of the external situation allows salespeople to be optimistic about their future sales and earnings opportunities. A shift from salary to incentive usually creates greater variation in earnings across salespeople. With more pay linked to performance, current top performers are likely to earn more money, average performers will earn about the same amount of money and poor performers will earn less. This makes it easier to gain the acceptance of current top performers, at least initially, but long-term acceptance depends on the sales force's risk profile. Salespeople who prefer the security of salary will worry about the loss of guaranteed income that comes with an increase in the incentive portion of pay.

Increasing the incentive portion of pay is particularly challenging when a completely salaried sales force converts to salary plus incentives for the first time. Even if the incentive portion of pay is small (15% or less), the move is a signal that the culture is changing. Similarly, it's difficult for a sales force with a low to moderate incentive (25% or less) to shift to a pay mix that includes the majority of earnings as incentives. In this case, salespeople must adjust their mindset as incentives become must-have rather than nice-to-have. In both of these situations, it's critical for management to communicate a convincing, well-supported case for change, along with a compelling outline of how the plan will look and feel in the future and how salespeople can succeed and benefit.

Even with a good communication plan, reducing salary will be difficult. Salespeople often view salary as an entitlement. Some specific strategies for gaining acceptance of a salary reduction include the following:

- **Eliminate merit raises instead of cutting salary.** Use the money saved to fund more incentive pay over a one- to three-year period until you reach the desired pay mix.

- **Provide a bridge period.** Guarantee the increased incentive amount during this period. Essentially, this means measuring and reporting on the new incentive pay amount without putting the pay truly at risk.

- **Consider offering recoverable income draws.** Recoverable draws (equal to some portion of the difference between the new and old salaries) can help salespeople adjust to the greater income swings they may experience pay period to pay period. Be prepared to manage some downsides of offering draws. A salesperson may owe the company money if his or her performance doesn't meet expectations. Also, draws can be costly to administer and can dilute the motivational power of incentives.

- **Show salespeople they can earn more money.** Demonstrate that, despite the salary cut, salespeople will earn more under the new plan as long as they exceed their sales quotas. For those who have struggled to make quota in the past, coach them on what they need to do differently to succeed in the future.

- **Show salespeople how much more they would have earned last year if the new pay mix had been in place.** Typically, your best salespeople would have made more money. Show additional upside earnings potential for increasing sales over last year's levels to enhance motivation further.

- **Remember that not everyone is motivated by money alone.** Demonstrating upside earnings potential may engage some salespeople, but others may respond better to other motivators, such as opportunities for interesting or meaningful work. Use a variety of sales force motivators to get the best results (see Chapter 5).

Implementing a Salary Portion Increase

Increases in salary are usually relatively easy to communicate provided the overall pay level stays the same. Strategies for addressing the challenges of increasing the salary portion of pay include the following:

- **Focus on keeping good salespeople.** Salespeople who thrive on the competition and drive for short-term results inherent in a high-incentive environment will most likely dislike an incentive pay reduction. Unfortunately, salespeople who are currently top earners are more likely to be unhappy, so the change could create undesired sales force turnover. Seek to protect and retain good salespeople, perhaps by giving them significant additional recognition or perks.

- **Consider a transition period.** Have a transition compensation plan so that salespeople who are important to the company's future are less likely to experience a sudden pay cut. For example, guarantee salespeople will make at least as much as they would have under last year's plan, or consider phasing in the change by moving a fraction of incentive pay into salary each year until the company reaches the desired mix.

- **Consider reducing total target pay to reflect the reduction in salespeople's risk.** Occasionally, when companies increase the guaranteed portion of pay, they may reduce total target pay in exchange for less risk for salespeople. For example, if salespeople's target pay was $100,000 at a 50:50 mix, the company will choose to set a target of $95,000 at a 70:30 mix. Doing this also helps to contain compensation costs when performance is down. Generally, a sales force will find any pay reduction demotivating, so make sure the reduction is felt most by below-average performers, and keep a keen focus on retaining good salespeople and key customers.

Changing Performance Metrics and Payout Formulas

Changes to performance metrics and payout formulas can come about as companies strive to keep incentives aligned with evolving sales strategies. For example:

- A company seeking to drive more profitable sales may modify its incentive plan metrics to pay on gross margin rather than on sales.

- A company trying to reinforce a team-oriented sales approach may add a team-based metric.

- A company trying to create more globally consistent sales force pay may develop global guidelines for incentive plan metrics and payout formulas. In order to conform to the guidelines, some countries may change their plan structure and adjust features such as commission accelerators and thresholds.

Changes to metrics and payout formulas are especially difficult to implement when they redistribute income opportunity among salespeople. Strategies for implementing such changes include the following:

- **Figure out who in the sales force is helped and who is hurt by the change.** This allows you to address concerns and seek to retain people who are important to the company's future. Figure 10-2 provides an example of an analysis a consumer packaged goods company conducted when it planned to change its incentive plan structure. The company used last year's performance data to calculate how much more or less money each salesperson would have earned had the proposed new plan been in place. In this case, approximately 55% of salespeople would have lost income under the new plan. The company confirmed almost all top performers were among the 45% of salespeople who would have gained income had the new plan been in place last year.

- **Show salespeople what they need to do differently to make the same (or more) incentive pay with a new plan.** For instance, when one company switched from a revenue-based to a gross-margin-based incentive plan metric, it provided an example showing salespeople who were in the top 10% of earnings with the old plan

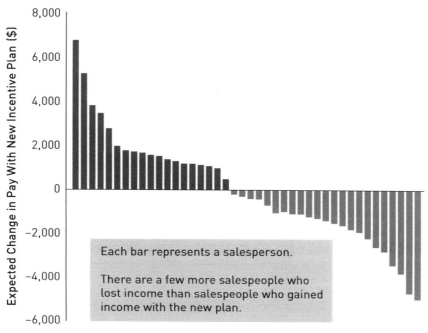

Figure 10-2. Who Is Helped and Who Is Hurt by Incentive Plan Change

how to stay in the top 10% with the new plan by changing the mix of products they sold and the price they offered. The company also provided an example for average performers demonstrating how to maintain and improve incentive earnings under the new plan. First-line sales managers played a key role in coaching salespeople on what to do differently to succeed under the new plan.

- **Consider a transition period.** Often, it's impossible to avoid hurting at least some top performers in the short term when metrics or payout formulas change. To avoid undesired turnover, consider a plan allowing salespeople to maintain their income level for a limited time while rebuilding their business for success under the new plan. Features can include retention bonuses, guarantees, dual plans, grandfathering and buyback arrangements, but these strategies should be used with caution and only for a short period.

- **Let salespeople preview new metrics.** When changing incentive plan metrics, incorporate a new metric into sales reporting and performance management processes three to 12 months before the metric becomes part of the incentive plan. This gives the sales force and the sales support group time to adjust. Inevitably, some exceptions and needed clarifications to the new metric will be discovered only after the metric is rolled out. For example, a new gross margin metric may create controversy about exactly how to account for changing product and distribution costs in the margin calculation. It's much easier to resolve an issue like this when salespeople's incentive pay is not at stake. You also can drop metrics that create excessive confusion, evoke undesirable sales force behaviors or compromise customer focus during the trial period.

Changing From a Commission Plan to a Quota-Based Plan

A particularly difficult transition is changing a commission plan paying from the first dollar sold to a quota-based plan paying only for sales above a quota or threshold. Companies may do this if pay levels under the commission plan start growing precipitously because salespeople are generating many repeat sales for minimal sales effort yet aren't serving their customers well or following up on all opportunities. Salespeople don't want to give up earning potential, so the company risks losing salespeople and customers if it changes the commission plan or tries to reassign accounts to improve customer coverage.

A biotechnology company used culture and communication to enable the transition from a commission plan to a quota-based plan without significant sales force and customer disruption. Back when the company had launched its first product, sales leaders had introduced an incentive plan paying salespeople a commission on all sales in their territory, while making it clear that the plan would change after the initial launch phase. By the second year after launch, the company had enough data to make reasonable forecasts of territory-level sales, and it changed to a quota-based incentive plan. Salespeople's payout started at 80% of their territory sales quota and accelerated beyond 100% of quota. Going forward, the company could adjust territory quotas as needed to keep pay levels in line with the evolving sales role and market needs.

By thinking ahead when creating a sales compensation plan, and using analytics to predict future financial consequences under different performance scenarios, companies can anticipate outcomes. Then by building flexibility into their plans and into their culture, they will have an easier time implementing changes as markets and company strategies evolve.

Reducing Total Sales Force Pay

Pressure to cut costs can force companies to reduce pay levels for many employees, including salespeople, to remain financially viable. Pay cuts specific to the sales force are rare but do occasionally occur. As more selling shifts to inside sales or online channels, the number of people in expensive sales roles will likely go down. Pay cuts are possible for some roles, especially when salespeople are paid well above the industry average and there is almost no turnover, particularly of mediocre performers.

Across-the-board pay cuts may involve reductions to salary, incentive pay or both. External market surveys are available in many industries for benchmarking both salary (fixed) and incentive (variable) pay for most sales roles.

There is no easy way to get the sales force to accept a pay cut. Be honest about why it's happening. Gaining sales force acceptance will be easier if the pay cut is driven by an urgent need (for example, the company is in financial trouble or is rapidly losing market share) rather than if it is based solely on the need to trim fat or to bring costs in line with industry norms.

If the pay cut makes your company's pay level less favorable than what alternative employers offer and your salespeople are in demand in the employment market, expect to lose some salespeople.

Consider the following strategies when implementing a sales force pay cut:

- **Focus on keeping key customers.** The circumstances prompting a pay cut may cause customers to worry about the company's financial health or about the salesperson assigned to their account leaving. Help customers understand you are looking out for their long-term interests and have a transition plan in place in case salespeople who have relationships with key customers leave.

- **Focus on keeping good salespeople.** Identify the salespeople you really want to keep, including current top performers and the salespeople who are most likely to be successful in the future. Seek to protect and retain these salespeople. Consider giving them additional responsibilities and enhancing their pay. By increasing the pay difference between top and bottom performers, you may be able to reduce the average pay level, while ensuring that top salespeople win even as others in the sales force lose.

- **Cut leadership's pay.** Let the sales force know everyone is sacrificing.

- **Focus on non-monetary motivators.** Use the opportunity to implement new non-monetary motivational programs and low-cost job improvements, such as reduced administrative requirements, to enhance retention.

- **Consider maintaining pay opportunity while requiring productivity improvements.** Make quotas more challenging to achieve, or tie incentive pay to a metric that is suffering. For example, if the sales force is cutting price to make revenue quotas, linking incentives to gross margin rather than revenue will require salespeople to work harder and smarter to earn the same pay.

- **Consider freezing pay levels.** Rather than cutting pay all at once, phase in cost reductions over time by eliminating raises.

- **Consider reducing the size of the sales force.** Instead of cutting pay, cut costs by eliminating poor performers and by offering a severance package encouraging some salespeople to take early retirement.

When the large financial service firm described earlier in this chapter reduced sales force pay by cutting commissions in half, it lost more than half its salespeople and a huge chunk of business. Several of the strategies just listed could have helped this firm avoid the tremendous loss. Certainly that firm would have been better positioned to avoid the loss had leaders anticipated how sales compensation costs were likely to grow.

Anticipation allowed a technology distributor to take steps today to avoid spiraling sales compensation costs in the future. The distributor paid salespeople mostly through commissions plus a small base salary. Financial projections showed this compensation model was not sustainable, given the growth the distributor sought for the future. Not wanting to upset current salespeople who were making a lot of money, the distributor grandfathered in the existing sales force while offering new salespeople a different, lower-cost compensation plan. This helped get sales compensation costs under control without disrupting the salespeople who controlled important customer relationships.

Smart use of resources in good times reduces the need for sales force pay cuts during bad times. Spend cautiously in successful years and use short-term incentives (a special good-year bonus or incentive trip), while making it clear these perks will not be offered in less successful years.

Focusing on Change Management

Implementing the major sales compensation and incentive plan changes often required in today's sales environment necessitates a thoughtful change management approach. Although minor compensation plan tweaks can be implemented in a few weeks at the end of the year, major changes such as the ones described in this chapter require a sustained focus on change management and implementation throughout the entire planning process. Change management should be part of the agenda at every planning meeting, starting with first one.

Some key steps for implementing major compensation and incentive plan change are outlined here.

Start by Understanding the Current State

Before redesigning sales compensation and incentives, use plan health checks (see Chapter 8) to gain a better understanding of the current state of your sales compensation program. In addition, information-gathering methods such as confidential sales force surveys and focus groups can enhance your understanding of salespeople's current knowledge, attitudes and preferences about sales compensation.

Consider engaging an advisory board of several high-performing salespeople whom others in the sales force respect and view as go-to people for advice. In addition to helping you assess the current state, these advisors can help plan an effective rollout process and persuasion plan and can influence the rest of the sales force by encouraging positive conversation about the change.

Recognize Stakeholder Perspectives and Design the Sales Force Experience

The company's perspective on why the sales compensation plan is changing is not necessarily the best perspective to share when persuading individual sales force members. Individuals want to know what's in it for them. For example, even though salespeople may understand on a rational level that the company is reducing upside incentive earning potential to save money and remain viable long term, no salesperson is likely to find such a reduction motivating.

Interestingly (and somewhat counterintuitively), gaining sales force acceptance of change is often easier when salespeople are in a situation in which they believe their success is threatened, such as when they are feeling the impact of an economic downturn or a competitive challenge. They are less likely to embrace change when it simply promises new opportunity – for example, when a new incentive plan provides greater opportunity to salespeople who sell more strategic products. This asymmetry in behavior – the willingness to accept change that avoids a certain level of loss and the reluctance to accept change that offers the same potential for gain – has implications for the best way to frame sales force communications about compensation plan change.

Before implementing a sales compensation change, put yourself in the sales force's shoes; consider engaging a small team of change champions from the sales force who can share perspective directly. Think about how the proposed changes will affect, negatively or positively, what salespeople care about on an emotional level. Anticipate salespeople's perceptions about what they will lose and what they could win.

Make a list of exciters, or experiences you'd like to create. This list might include a compelling and credible benefit for sales force members, success stories from peers and the incorporation of sales force and customer input into the plan design process.

At the same time, make a list of downers, or experiences you'd like to avoid. This list might include the perception of no clear benefit to salespeople, a lack of sales manager support and excessive complexity in the new plan. Use this information to inform the persuasion process, and design a stakeholder engagement plan that involves the right people in the right ways.

Create a Change Management Team

A cross-functional team should have specific responsibility for change management and persuading the sales force. The team should have clear objectives, strong support from senior leadership, sufficient time and budget and accountability for successful implementation.

Typical participants can include the leader of the sales force, a leader from sales operations, regional directors or managers (or a few selected ones), and participants from departments such as human resources and information technology. A few salesperson advisors can be valuable team contributors as well, provided the company is willing to reveal in advance that it plans to change sales compensation.

Develop a Persuasion Plan

Never underestimate the time and effort needed to develop a plan for communicating compensation and incentive plan changes to the sales force. Create communication materials with concise messages by using plain language and visuals. Share specific examples showing how incentive pay is calculated and what salespeople need to do differently to succeed under the new plan.

Have a detailed rollout process for the initial announcement and for cascading the information down through the sales ranks, as well as for ongoing communication. Use a mix of communication channels, including face-to-face discussions, conference calls, intranet message boards and e-newsletters. After the first paycheck, a town-hall-style question-and-answer session over the telephone or the sharing of tips and success stories on the company's intranet can go a long way in driving adoption of the new plan.

Ensure Leaders and Managers Are Engaged in Constant Communication

Persuasive and consistent communication from sales leadership at events such as national sales meetings, weekly teleconferences, regional meetings and field visits is critical for helping salespeople understand and embrace change. In addition, first-line sales managers play an important role in gaining salespeople's acceptance. Managers are the first source of information for salespeople and the conduit for change, so it is critical that managers can understand and explain the program. In addition to sharing the reasons for the change, managers can coach salespeople on new metrics and what to do differently with customers to succeed under the new plan. Managers also help to keep the team energized by providing encouragement and celebrating early successes.

Conclusion

Forces in today's sales environment are creating a need for some companies to make major sales compensation and incentive plan changes, including pay mix changes and incentive plan metric and payout formula modifications that potentially redistribute income among salespeople. Without careful attention to implementation and persuading the sales team, such changes can create significant sales force and customer disruption. The challenge is especially great for companies in change-unfriendly situations – where there is considerable risk of losing salespeople and customers.

It's critical for companies facing major compensation and incentive plan changes to invest sufficient time and energy to ensuring changes are implemented well and are understood and accepted by the sales force. A good incentive compensation plan design that is well implemented will almost always outperform a great plan design that is poorly implemented.

A carefully planned implementation and persuasion approach is essential for bringing about the change required to keep your sales compensation plan aligned with your sales strategy, while retaining the high-performing salespeople you can't afford to lose.

Index

About the Authors

 **Andris (Andy) Zoltners** is the Frederic Esser Nemmers Distinguished Professor Emeritus of Marketing at the Kellogg School of Management at Northwestern University, where he has been a faculty member for more than 30 years. In 1983, Andy cofounded the sales and marketing consulting firm ZS with Prabha Sinha. The company's global success was recognized by their induction into the Chicago Area Entrepreneurship Hall of Fame in 2005. Andy has consulted personally for companies around the world, helping them implement strategies and programs that drive results. In addition to his consulting, Andy has taught sales force topics to thousands of executive, M.B.A. and Ph.D. students. He is the coauthor of numerous academic articles, blogs for the *Harvard Business Review,* and a series of books on sales force management. He received his Ph.D. from Carnegie-Mellon University.

 **Prabhakant (Prabha) Sinha** cofounded the sales and marketing consulting firm ZS with Andy Zoltners in 1983. The company's global success was recognized by their induction into the Chicago Area Entrepreneurship Hall of Fame in 2005. Prabha was an Associate Professor of Marketing at the Kellogg School of Management at Northwestern University until 1987 and continues to teach sales executives at the Gordon Institute of Business Science in South Africa and the Indian School of Business. He has consulted personally for firms all over the world, helping them improve sales force strategy and effectiveness. He is the coauthor of numerous academic articles, blogs for the *Harvard Business Review,* and a series of books on sales force management. Prabha received his Ph.D. from the University of Massachusetts and graduated from the Indian Institute of Technology Kharagpur.

Chad Albrecht is a Principal at ZS and is a leader in the firm's Sales Compensation Practice. Chad, a Certified Sales Compensation Professional, has more than 20 years of consulting experience with Hewitt Associates and ZS. He has helped clients create and implement motivational sales incentive plans and set fair and challenging sales quotas in industries that include high tech, hospitality, business services, pharmaceuticals, medical devices, telecom, distribution and manufacturing. He is the author of several articles in industry publications, a regular speaker at conferences, a frequent contributor to ZS's blog *The Carrot,* and the coauthor of *The Future of Sales Compensation.*

Steve Marley is a Principal at ZS. As a leader in the firm's Sales Compensation Practice, he oversees ZS's Sales Performance Management work. Steve, a Certified Sales Compensation Professional, has more than 10 years of consulting experience spanning industries including software, distribution, financial services, pharmaceuticals and medical devices. He has helped companies design effective compensation plans, set motivating quotas and implement efficient compensation administration programs. His current focus is helping companies transition from thinking about monetary incentives to thinking holistically about motivation, engagement and incentives. Steve is a frequent contributor to ZS's blog *The Carrot,* and is the coauthor of *The Future of Sales Compensation.*

Sally Lorimer is a business writer and a former Principal at ZS, where she helped clients implement strategies for improving sales effectiveness and performance. She is the coauthor of numerous academic articles, blogs for the *Harvard Business Review,* and a series of books on sales force management. She has an M.B.A. from the Kellogg School of Management at Northwestern University and is also a graduate of the Stephen M. Ross School of Business at the University of Michigan.

Also Written by the Authors

The Future of Sales Compensation

Chad Albrecht | Steve Marley

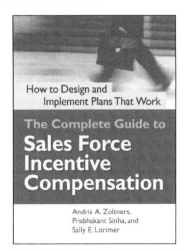

How to Design and Implement Plans That Work

The Complete Guide to Sales Force Incentive Compensation

Andris A. Zoltners,
Prabhakant Sinha, and
Sally E. Lorimer

POWERFUL STRATEGIES FOR DRIVING HIGH PERFORMANCE

BUILDING A WINNING SALES FORCE

Andris A. Zoltners = Prabhakant Sinha = Sally E. Lorimer

The Power of Sales Analytics

ANDRIS A. ZOLTNERS | PRABHAKANT SINHA | SALLY E. LORIMER

Building a Winning Sales Management Team

The Force Behind the Sales Force

Andris A. Zoltners | Prabhakant Sinha | Sally E. Lorimer
ZS Associates

Insights for Sales Force Success

Practical Ideas for Winning in Today's Sales Environment

ANDRIS A. ZOLTNERS
PRABHA K. SINHA
SALLY E. LORIMER

Subscribe to *The Carrot* Blog!

Stay on Top of Trends and Best Practices in Sales Compensation

Written by **the world's leading sales compensation experts**, ZS Principals Steve Marley, Chad Albrecht and Mike Martin, *The Carrot* is a must-read for leaders who want real-world insights on current sales compensation issues.

Subscribe today and receive tips, tricks and best practices for designing, implementing and managing sales compensation plans that drive performance.

www.zs.com/thecarrot